A FABIAN/UNISON SPECIAL

jobs and GROWTH

THE INTERNATIONAL PERSPECTIVE

Edited by Stephen Pollard

Supported by

Fabian Society (GB)
Friedrich Ebert Foundation (Germany)
Center for Policy Alternatives (US)
Economic Policy Institute (US)
UNISON (GB)

This book was made possible by
a generous donation from
The Webb Memorial Trust.

The Oxford seminar was helped by a grant from
The German Marshall Fund of the US.

i

Jobs and growth: the international perspective

This book, like all publications of the Fabian Society, represents not the collective views of the Society but only the views of the authors. The responsibility of the Society is limited to approving its publications as worthy of consideration within the Labour movement.

Design: Tony Garrett

November 1994

ISBN 0 7163 4019 4

ISSN 0307 7523

Printed by The College Hill Press Limited (TU), London and Worthing

Published by the Fabian Society, 11 Dartmouth St., London SW1H 9BN

Preface

Jacques Delors

The strength of this book is the vigorous debate
it encourages on practical measures to tackle the
high levels of unemployment and poverty that
disfigure all the advanced economies. It is a
counterattack against the failing neo-liberal
model of the unrestrained free market.

I share its assumptions that full employment must be the centrepiece of a
decent society; that governments have a vital role in achieving full
employment; that social partnership remains a necessary instrument of
social progress; and that trade unionism continues to be an important
means of organising and mobilising ordinary people.

There are no miracle cures. The globalisation of the economy, the emergence
of new competitors, exploiting comparative advantages in working conditions
and costs, and continuous levels of unemployment of around 10%, raise profound questions about our ability to reorder our priorities and renew our
institutions.

But I refuse to accept that economic decline is inevitable: I believe we will
find new forms of sustainable growth capable of generating millions of jobs. Nor
should we accept the unacceptable: the idea of solidarity lies at the heart of a
new deal, and all of us must strive for a less partial view of humanity.

I welcome the debate opened by this book in its analyses, its ideas and its
call to action.

The only real issue

Stephen Pollard

There is only one real economic issue facing the western world – what to do about unemployment. So used have we now become to levels which were inconceivable twenty years ago, that unemployment is seen almost as a natural phenomenon. When we are lucky it is slightly lower but, realistically, it is beyond our control.

This rejection of responsibility is, of course, nonsense. For one thing, the Conservative governments in the UK have, despite their rhetoric, shown the impact that government policy can have – from Lord Howe's wilful savaging of the British economy in the early 1980s, cutting manufacturing output by 20% and adding 2 million to unemployment, to Lord Lawson's huge credit, property and consumer booms, large and unsustainable enough to make the South Sea Bubble look like a well-founded investment decision. The 1980s, even more than the 1950s and '60s the era of 'stop-go' economics, shows, above all else, that government policy matters.

As Andrew Graham points out in his overview of the post-War years in Chapter 2, for three decades we did combine full employment with price stability. Not because it happened to come right but because the 1944 White Paper willed it to come right by accepting not only that the government had a duty to work for full employment but that it also had the power. And yet since the oil price shocks of the 1970s and the consequent monetarist hegemony, public discussion of economics has seemed to disregard the traditional goals of policy such as growth and employment – except, of course, for price stability. But the other goals are not only as valid now as ever, they are almost more important, as western societies suffer from the economic and social effects of large scale human waste.

Training

Because of this falling away of belief in the power of government, we have had to find another message. The Lord is one, and the word was 'training'. Training has become the big idea on which all our hopes are built. It is, unquestionably, a good thing. It is wholesome. It shows we understand fears of an undereducated generation. But it is also like the emperor's new clothes: no one listens to the person who points out that training creates neither jobs or growth. Training does not create anything except trainees. Indeed, recent evidence puts paid to the idea that Britain's failure successfully to compete with Germany is a product of our failure properly to train those below degree level. Productivity growth in manufacturing in Britain and Germany has been boosted significantly by degree level skills, but not since the mid-1970s by intermediate skills[1].

Power to act

There are lessons to be learnt from contrasting post-War experiences. First, we need to recapture a belief in our power to affect the economy for the better. And then we have to persuade the electorate that things will get better. For any party of the Left, a belief in the potential of government to enable progress and improvement is a prerequisite of electoral success.

But before we can do any of that, we have to know what we want to do in government.

Rich Ferlauto in Chapter 8 makes the important point that in the US many important economic decisions are taken at the local level. With the European Union increasingly becoming, for good or ill, a 'Europe of the Regions', the potential of the ideas he outlines must be taken on board across the Union, and are as relevant in countries such as the UK with a high degree of centralisation as they are in those such as Germany with a more devolved system of government.

Jeff Faux argues persuasively in Chapter 3 that the 'success' of the so-called American model – characterised by deregulation, weak unions and a minimal welfare state – which governments across the world have sought to replicate, in creating more jobs, lowering labour costs and restructuring firms which are then better able to compete on the world market, is illusory. The British experience – spending the last fifteen years moving steadily towards the American Model and getting not so much steadily as joltingly worse – is proof that this is no way forward.

So what do we want instead? Chris Boyd and John Evans in Chapters 5 and 6 paint two sides of the European coin: the Delors White Paper which, for all the questions it begs, is a symbol that concerted European action is taken seriously on one level; and the issues raised by deregulation of labour – or 'flexibility' in the language of some.

New currents

There are signs that the intellectual current is begining to swing back towards this more appealing model, based on firm evidence that it actually works. The idea, for instance, so beloved of the Right, that labour is no more than a commodity which operates by the classical laws of supply and demand, has been shown to be empirically untrue by two British economists, David Blanchflower and Andrew Oswald[2]. Examining the relation between wages and unemployment in 12 countries (as varied as Germany, the US and South Korea), they show that, rather than low wages correlating with low local unemployment and high wages with high local unemployment, in fact the opposite is true. It is simply not the case, as the evidence shows, that the unemployed in an area of high unemployment bid down the wages of those in work. The free market theorists' levelling off of wages to a lower market clearing rate simply does not happen. As Robert Solow argues, it would not be rational for unemployed workers to bid down wage rates since they would be depressing their potential level of future earnings. And although theory would have it that a minimum wage would cut employment as companies were unable to afford the cost of taking as many people on, the evidence shows that a minimum wage can create jobs. Without a minimum wage, employers may pay employees less than the value of their work because the opportunity cost of looking for alternative employment is too high for it to be worthwhile. Thus, a minimum wage above what employers want to pay but below what workers are worth will encourage more people to apply for jobs, and it will still be profitable to take them on[3].

In a similar challenge to received opinion, Linda Tarr-Whelan in Chapter 7 shows how the increasing participation rates of women in the workforce is not a *problem*, reducing the number of jobs available to men, but is an *opportunity* for economic growth. Once again, the figures spell out the truth.

But of course there is a more obvious refutation of free market economics – the persistence of high rates of unemployment across the western world, exposing the sham of the supposed self-regulating tendencies of the system to move back to full employment of its own accord. Leaving it to the market empirically does not work. Some economists could usefully learn that reality is often different from the prejudices they call theory.

Part of the reason for the defeatism which has bred so many economic eunuchs has been the Left's failure successfully to compete with the Right in its attempt to create a sympathetic intellectual and popular climate. While the Right meet regularly across the world, on the Left, although theoretically more internationalist, we tend to talk only to each other. But the transparent failure of the Right's project has instilled a new sense of purpose in some on the Left. That is why for the first time ever a group drawn from progressive think tanks, universities and unions from across Europe, Australia, Canada and the US met in April 1994 at the 'International Seminar on Growth and Employment' held in Magdalen College, Oxford. This book is a product of that meeting.

A welcome theme which emerged at the seminar was the importance of Keynesian – or 'neo-Keynesian', if it makes some people happier – ideas. The macro, as Bob Kuttner outlines in Chapter 4, has (in theory if not yet in practice) made a long-overdue comeback. As the concluding chapter – the Rapporteurs' Report of the Magdalen seminar – by Bob Kuttner and Will Hutton puts it: "The remedy will require...Keynesian policies to restore higher levels of investment, productivity, growth and purchasing power".

Only by an awareness of each others' projects and work can we hope to repeat the success of the Right in changing world opinion. The seminar marked a first step. This book is a second. For a third, we wait for the next gathering in Washington D.C.

References
[1]National Institute for Economic and Social Research, cited by Robert Chote, *Independent on Sunday,* 12th June 1994
[2]Blanchflower and Oswald, *The Wage Curve, Journal of Economic Perspectives,* MIT Press
[3]Robert Chote, *Independent on Sunday*, 12th June 1994

Did Keynesianism work?

2

Andrew Graham

In the famous 1944 White Paper, the British Government committed the United Kingdom to pursue full employment in the post-war period. Soon after this publication full employment was defined as 3% of the working population and it hardly ever exceeded this level for the next thirty years. It is therefore tragic that fifty years later unemployment in the UK in the last few years has averaged nearly three times that level. Indeed, since 1973 it has never been below 3%.

The UK is not alone. Almost all industrialised countries exhibit a similar pattern with low unemployment until half way through the 1970s and high unemployment thereafter. Now, in 1994, unemployment throughout the industrialised world is at its highest ever in the post-war level, totalling some 35 million people; and the OECD estimate that, on top of this, there are another 15 million who have either given up looking for work or have unwillingly accepted a part-time job.

The obvious questions which arise are: why has this happened and what can be done about it? Answers to such large questions can necessarily only be painted in broad strokes. The structure of this chapter is therefore as follows. First, there is a survey of the broad trends of employment, output and unemployment in the post-war period. Then the chapter focuses on two questions raised by these trends: did Keynesian demand management policies contribute to low unemployment up to 1973; and, if so, why were such policies subsequently abandoned? The next section looks at lessons that might be learnt and the conclusion draws out the policy implications.

Employment, output, unemployment

The basic picture is shown in Table 1. As is well known, output throughout the industrialised world during the 'Golden Age' of 1950-1973 grew at a faster rate than at any other time in history. Since then the rate of growth of output has returned to a level similar to that of the preceding century. Alongside this, unemployment in the Golden Age stayed at abnormally low levels, whereas after 1973 unemployment has risen in almost all countries. Equally well known, the recession of 1990-1994 has slowed growth further and pushed unemployment to record levels.

Table 1: OECD Employment, output and unemployment

	Employment (% change p. a.)	Output (% change p. a.)	Unemployment[a] (End of Period)
1870-1950	0.9	2.4	3.4[b]
1950-1973	1.2	4.9	3.2[c]
1973-1990	1.2	2.7	6.3[d]
1990-1993	- 0.2	1.2	9.1[e]

(a) Arithmetical average percentage rate of US, Japan, Germany, France, Italy, UK, Canada, Belgium, Netherlands, Norway, Sweden and Australia.

(b) Average 1950/51

(c) Average 1972/73

(d) Average 1989/90s

(e) Average 1993/94

(Source: Maddison[1] and OECD)

Possibly less well known are the figures on employment. With output slowing down so sharply, employment growth might also have been expected to be slower. This did not occur. As Table 1 shows, the rate of growth of employment was just as fast from 1973 to 1990 as before 1973. This is because the decline in the rate of growth of output was totally matched by a decline in the rate of growth of productivity. However, even though jobs were created just as fast, unemployment increased. There must, therefore, have been a large increase in the labour force.

Lying behind these aggregate figures are some equally striking changes in the gender and sectoral mix of the labour force. In many countries the rise in the labour force has been composed largely of an increase in the participation rate of women, and many of these women have contributed to the rapid growth of employment in the service sector. At the same time there has been a decline in employment in manufacturing and, as a result, a rise in male unemployment.

Even in a summary account of the post-war period two other features stand out. First, in addition to the obvious cyclical movement of unemployment there appears to have been an upward trend. In each recession unemployment has climbed higher and in each recovery the fall in unemployment has been less.

Second, there have been significant differences between countries. In particular, during the 1980s employment has risen far more rapidly in the US than in Europe. On the other hand, the rise in employment in the US has been at the expense of greatly increased inequality in the distribution of earnings (though, as Table 2 shows, there is no general correlation between rapid increases in employment and high levels of wage inequality, nor between increases in employment and increases in inequality).

Table 2: Wage inequality and employment growth

| | Wage Inequality[a] | | Employment |
	Mid 70s/ Early 80s	Late 80s Early 90s	Growth 1982-92
USA	4.7	5.6	+20.1
UK	2.4	3.4	+4.0
France	3.2	3.2	+4.4
Japan	2.6	2.8	+14.3
Austria	2.6	2.7	+9.5
Belgium[b]	2.4	2.3	+6.4
Germany[c]	2.4	2.3	+7.8
Netherlands	2.0	2.3	+17.2
Denmark[b]	2.1	2.2	+7.3
Sweden	2.1	2.2	+3.2
Italy	2.0	2.0	+4.7
Norway[b]	2.1	2.0	+3.5

(a) Male wages; ratio of upper to lower decile

(b) Males and females

(c) West Germany to 1991, all Germany thereafter

(Source: OECD Employment Outlook)

All three of these factors – the variation between countries, the sectoral and gender variation and, above all, the trend rise in unemployment – have led many commentators to argue that most, possibly all, unemployment is structural. What we are observing, it is argued, is either a mismatch between job opportunities and the skills available or labour markets where the wages are insufficiently flexible. If so, what is required is yet further reform on the supply side of the economy.

The alternative view is that the decline in the rate of growth of output, and to some extent the slower growth in productivity, are the result of successive recessions brought about by inadequate demand. In this case what would be required to tackle unemployment would be action on the demand side of the economy not the supply side.

Of course, these two views need not be in conflict. Structural unemployment could easily co-exist with cyclical unemployment. More interestingly, there is the possibility that what begins as cyclical unemployment can easily be transformed over time into structural unemployment (a point to which I return below).

Nevertheless, whatever the balance between these two views, what is striking about the past is the extent to which unemployment appeared to have been cured during the Golden Age. Anyone wishing to tackle unemployment at the present must therefore begin by asking why we were so much more successful in the past.

Keynesian policies and the Golden Age

The most striking fact about Keynesian policies is the straight-forward coincidence of the use of such policies and their success. During the period when these policies were most used unemployment was low and growth was high. In contrast, in the pre-Keynesian 1930s mass unemployment had been the norm, and in the post-Keynesian 1980s and 1990s unemployment and slow growth have re-emerged.

Theoretical considerations reinforce the conclusion that Keynesian policies contributed significantly to the success of the 1950s and 1960s. Keynesianism provided both an explanation of unemployment and offered a means to control it and, in the eyes of almost all the observers at the time, the governments of the day *were* using Keynesian policies and *were* achieving the results that theory predicted. This was especially so in the US and the UK, then the two most powerful countries in the world; the two countries where the Keynesian intellectual revolution had been most profound and the two countries which most clearly committed themselves to full employment at the end of the war.

Of course, as is now well known, later observers have questioned this view. Matthews[2], in particular, showed that British budget deficits were actually smaller in the 1950s than in the 1930s and argued that this was, prima facie, inconsistent with Keynesian policies having been used. But in my view Matthews' results display the power of Keynesianism, not its weakness. By the mid-1950s the success of Keynesianism was so much taken for granted that the private sector expected full employment to be the norm. As a result private sector demand was high and for most of the time extra stimulation by the government not required. Moreover, even when a stimulus was needed, a small prod was sufficient. In short, the real power of Keynesian policies was in generating expectations of full employment and economic growth - expectations that were, by and large, self-fulfilling

No impartial observer of this period would, however, argue that Keynesian policies were solely responsible for the success of the Golden Age. There were a great many facilitating factors. First, the memories of the 1930s and the strong political desire to avoid returning to unemployment and protectionism generated a political consensus in favour of Keynesianism.

Second, the gradual removal of trade barriers and the enormous expansion of international trade undoubtedly aided rapid economic growth. It did so both by facilitating international specialisation and by generating greater competitive pressure to raise productivity.

Third, the European economy had plentiful supplies of labour. These came not only externally from immigration, but also internally as agricultural productivity rose and labour was transferred first to manufacturing and then to services.

All of these facilitating factors created a climate in which economic growth not only *seemed* possible but *was* possible. As a result, increases in money wages were almost entirely matched by increases in productivity, and inflation was low. Although the success in containing inflation varied from country to country in ways dependent on the degree of social consensus and the structure of wage bargaining, for the most part workers' desires for higher standards of living were met without unions having to be aggressive.

Yet Keynesianism was a crucial part of this successful jigsaw. The structural change associated with the expansion of trade only occurred because, within the context of full employment, there were always new jobs to go to. Thus Keynesianism, free trade, rapid growth, an easy labour supply and the political consensus to intervene when necessary generated a virtuous circle.

Inflation and the balance of payments

All of this is relatively well known. What is less well recognised is that this period was quite abnormal in being relieved of both the inflation constraint at the world level and the balance of payments constraint. These are the two dogs that did not bite during the golden period. Why not?

The fundamental point about world inflation is that throughout the years 1952-1972 the world economy was out of phase. As Figure 1 shows, during the 1950s, when Europe was expanding rapidly, America was moving slowly away from full capacity. Then in the 1960s, as the American economy boomed, the Europeans slowed down. As a result, commodity prices were unusually stable throughout the whole period 1952-1972. In contrast, at the very beginning of this period the Korean war of 1951-52 pushed up commodity prices because of the rearmament boom. Similarly, at the end of the period in the first coincident peace time boom of 1972-1973, commodity prices again rose rapidly, pushing inflation up in all the industrialised countries. But these are the exceptions that prove the rule. For nearly twenty years in between, inflation was remarkably low, especially given the low level of unemployment that was sustained.

Figure 1: The economic cycle – Europe and the US, 1952-73

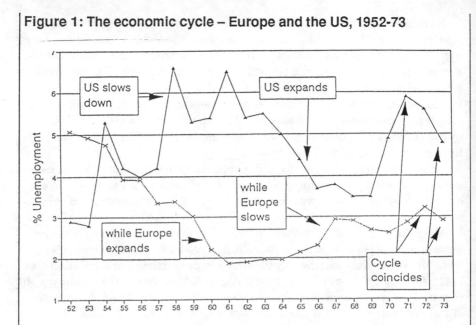

The fact that the world economy moved in this non-coincident manner was almost entirely good luck. It was certainly not the result of conscious international macroeconomic policy coordination.

The second piece of good fortune during the Golden Age was the development of the international monetary system. Many people are under the impression that the system of trade and payments established at Bretton Woods ran relatively successfully from its inception in 1944 to its collapse in 1971. This is far from the truth. The system would have collapsed on a number of occasions if there had not been later policy interventions or particularly fortunate developments, none of which were foreseen in 1944. Four stand out.

First, there was the sterling crisis of 1947. The Bank of England, following the prescription of Bretton Woods, tried to make sterling convertible but the experiment lasted a mere six weeks before exchange controls had to be reimposed. Indeed, sterling did not become fully convertible until 1958 and the UK only finally abandoned all exchange controls in 1979.

Second, the expansion and recovery of the European economy after the war would have been halted in the late 1940s by a shortage of external finance if it had not been for Marshall Aid. The need for this was neither foreseen at the time at Bretton Woods nor part of the payments system then planned.

Third, by the late 1950s the world economy had swung from a dollar shortage of the 1940s to a dollar surplus. As a result, there was a plentiful supply of international liquidity which underpinned the expansion of international trade. Yet again this was a factor not foreseen by the creators of Bretton Woods.

10

Fourth, following the devaluations of 1949 and the rapid increases in productivity in Germany, Japan, France and Italy, all of these countries became highly competitive. As a result, they were able to combine rapid economic growth with balance of payments surpluses (the opposite of what standard theory would have predicted).

The joint effect of these four factors was largely to remove the balance of payments as a constraint on European expansion for the whole period from the end of the war until the late 1960s.

One other consequence of this particular pattern of development is worth noting. Some of the critics of Keynesianism argue that the countries which performed best (especially Germany and Japan and also France after 1958) seemed to use Keynesianism least. If so, they ask, why should Keynesianism be credited with so much success? However, once we remember these countries' incipient export surpluses, it is obvious that they had *no need* to stimulate demand domestically. In short, the success of Germany, Japan and France without Keynesianism does not disprove it. On the contrary, it shows the success it was having *elsewhere*. Without a high level of demand in the world economy as a whole these countries would not have been able to run persistent trade surpluses. The contrast with the 1930s makes the point most sharply. In the 1930s devaluations exported unemployment and invited retaliation; in the postwar period international competitiveness permitted growth and encouraged others.

The collapse of the Keynesian consensus

If the world economy worked so well within the context of a Keynesian consensus, why did this collapse?

The fundamental reason for the collapse of Keynesian methods of demand management was inflation. The electorate had been led to believe that Keynesianism could control both inflation and unemployment. So when both appeared together in the form of stagflation, Keynesianism seemed a failure.

The years 1974-1976 were the turning point in the UK. The explosion of inflation in 1975 was taken as evidence of a clear rebuttal of Keynesian theory. So rapidly and powerfully did opinions swing that, less than a year after the Chancellor of the Exchequer, Denis Healey, had been vigorously defending demand management by the UK and urging it on other countries, James Callaghan, the then Labour Prime Minister, went to the Labour Party Conference of 1976 and told delegates that "you cannot spend your way out of recession".

The total collapse of the Keynesian conventional wisdom cannot, however, be explained just by inflation. Two other related factors, one empirical and political, the other theoretical, compounded the effect.

First, the inflation of the 1970s was largely the result of increases in costs. This cost-based inflation not only squeezed profits but was also seen by the electorate as being largely the result of trade union pressure. The political effect was a dramatic change in the demands of the electorate and, as a result, in the objectives of government policy. Control of unemployment was no longer the top priority. What mattered was the control of inflation and the restoration of profitability. As much as anything else, it is this change in the objectives of economic policy which brought about the apparent collapse of Keynesian policies. Keynesian policy was supposed to solve unemployment but when control of inflation became the priority the very same policies were used to create unemployment!

Second, there was a theoretical revolution. This occurred because the Keynesianism that had been taught in most universities in the post-war period was far too mechanistic and simple-minded and thus stood on very flimsy foundations. The IS/LM model, with a Phillips curve added on to explain the labour market, dominated the economics profession during the 1950s and 1960s. At this time most economists were 'Keynesian' in their macroeconomic thinking and yet neo-classical in their microeconomics. This model allowed them to combine these two beliefs. Nevertheless the model had one very odd implication. Keynesian results could only be achieved in the long run if money illusion persisted. In other words, Keynesian unemployment depended on the special case of sticky money wages. If it were not for this, Keynes, it seemed, would have been a classical economist – so much, the critics said, for the Keynesian revolution and his claims to a *General* Theory.

Of course, in the 1950s and early 1960s this did not seem too worrying. Money wages were fairly sticky. As a result, even if Keynes' economics did rest on a special case, it happened to be the case that applied to the real world. Moreover, if Phillips were to be believed, there was a level of unemployment, only a little higher than the UK was then experiencing, at which money wages (or, to be more precise, unit costs) would be constant. In short the neo-Keynesians were content to live with a theory that looked a bit shaky and which used inconsistent assumptions (money illusion is irrational, yet micro theory is built on the postulate of the rational utility maximiser) as long as it seemed to work.

Seen from this perspective, the collapse of 'Keynesian' economics in the face of the inflation and unemployment of the 1970s is very understandable. Once the assumption of sticky money wages no longer applied to reality – as it certainly did not after 1975 – Keynesian theory was useless. Or so it seemed.

At the level of theory a single article did most of the damage. In 1975, Milton Friedman gave his IEA lecture "Unemployment versus Inflation?"[3]. This displayed more graphically than anything before that the Phillips curve was purely a short-run phenomenon. According to Friedman, the reason – the *only* reason – that could cause unemployment to fall as demand was expanded was that prices rose and in the short run workers were fooled and so real wages fell. It was therefore worthwhile for firms to take on extra workers. However, once workers realised what was happening, money wages would go up to compensate for the rise in prices and unemployment would go back to its previous "natural" level. Thus in the long run there was no trade-off between unemployment and inflation and the Phillips curve was vertical. Demand management policy was therefore useless.

World lessons

The consequence of this collapse of Keynesian economics and the monetarist counter-revolution that followed produced some highly paradoxical results. The first example is the interpretation that has been placed on the recession of 1974-1976. At that time the oil price rise imposed by the OPEC countries acted exactly like a huge international indirect tax. What is more, the transfer of this tax to the desert Arab countries, who could not spend it all, meant that in Keynesian terms there had been a large 'leakage' from the international economy. To offset this an equivalent 'injection' somewhere else was required. But this did not occur, resulting in large-scale unemployment. In other words, Keynesian macroeconomics, when transferred to the international level, can explain both the inflation (from the oil price rise) *and* the unemployment (less demand following the leakage). Yet in the popular imagination the unemployment is ascribed to a failure *of* Keynesianism rather than to a failure to *use* Keynesian policies.

The same happened with explanations of the recession of 1979-1982. Here again there was the Keynesian effect of a large oil price rise reducing aggregate demand. Then, on top of this, in the US, and even more so in the UK, monetary and fiscal policies were tightened and, as Keynesians would have predicted (and indeed did predict), a large recession resulted. Yet much of the academic literature, by now dominated by models of rational expectations in which government intervention had no real effects, largely failed to predict the recession and, when it occurred, treated it as a supply shock rather than a demand shock. The obvious Keynesian explanation, having become unfashionable, was largely ignored.

One other aspect of the recession of 1979-82 is worth noting. Most students of economics are taught about the Keynesian multiplier. However, within a week or so of learning about it they are also taught that, because there are leakages into imports and leakages into taxation, the overall multiplier is rather small and so, in practice, unimportant. But consider 1979-82 and two important changes occur. First, the relevant unit of analysis is not a single country but the world. Thus imports are no longer a leakage. Second, the major countries were aiming to balance their budgets, so net taxes are also no longer a leakage. As a result, the relevant multiplier is much larger. This factor is, I suggest, one reason why the 1979 recession went deeper and was more drawn out than most economists predicted (an argument that I made, in advance, at the time[4].

We must, however, be careful. It is not part of my argument that the whole of the post-war period can be explained in Keynesian terms, let alone in the unreconstructed Keynesianism of the early text books. Care is particularly necessary on four points: on the supply side, on the globalisation of financial markets, on the role of expectations and on inflation.

In the case of supply some of the disturbances of the 1970s and 1980s undoubtedly did reduce the aggregate capacity of the economy. The most obvious evidence of this is the persistent upward trend in unemployment. The gradual emergence of this higher level of structural unemployment has undoubtedly reduced the ability of demand management to reduce unemployment. However, it does not follow from this that demand management is irrelevant – a point to which I return below.

The second problem is the globalisation of financial markets. It is now a matter of only a few seconds before developments in one country are transmitted world-wide. As a result, exchange rates and interest rates are certainly out of the control of any single country. Moreover, in 1994 we have experienced one of the largest ever rises in medium term interest rates (an increase of about 50% from about 6% at the end of 1993 to about 9% now). It is therefore questionable whether these medium/long interest rates are within the control of even a *group* of countries acting in concert.

Interacting with these problems in financial markets are the extra difficulties caused by expectations and, in particular, what Allsopp[5] describes as the problem of controlling non-minimum phase systems. Imagine balancing a broomstick in your hand. To shift the top of the broom to the right it is necessary to move your hand at the bottom to the left and then, once the top is moving, to 'catch' it by moving your hand smartly to the right and slightly beyond the top. Fiscal policy has the same difficulty at or near the bottom of the recession. In order to get a public deficit down the economy has to recover but to make the economy recover, the deficit has to go up! Moreover, once the expectations of recovery set in, fiscal policy may well have to be tightened by more than it was loosened.

This 'broomstick' problem can interact with the financial markets in two ways. Those in the markets who do not understand non-minimum phase systems may take fright when policy goes in apparently the 'wrong' direction. Others, some understanding the complexities and some not, may doubt whether politically the broom will be caught later on. The example set in the UK by a series of Conservative Chancellors (Maudling in 1964, Barber in 1973 and Lawson in 1988), each of whom started a boom and then failed to slow it down, is not encouraging for those of us who believe that demand management can be run intelligently.

Finally there is the problem of inflation. The central point here is that Keynes said rather little about inflation in the context of high levels of unemployment. The fundamental Keynesian insight was to realise that the determination of nominal national income (PY) is determined by the decentralised decisions of savers, on the one hand and investors on the other. Moreover, according to Keynes, there is no reason why these decentralised decisions would produce a stable level of nominal income. However, the split of this nominal income between real output and inflation remained an open question.

The conclusion of this line of argument is that it is rather likely that the more inflationary the environment, the more any Keynesian stimulus will show up in inflation and the less benefit it will produce to output. In this important sense the ability of Keynesian policies to produce useful outcomes did decline sharply in the 1970s and the 1980s. However, by the same token, with inflation now so much lower and unemployment so much higher in the 1990s, it is time to re-examine the relevance of Keynesian policies and to see what lessons can be learned.

Lessons

The first lesson looking back at the last 50 years of economic history is that Keynesian economics was, and is, a demand story and not a labour market story. Above all, Keynesian unemployment does *not* depend on sticky wages but on inadequate demand. As a result, both the Phillips Curve and Friedman's subsequent attack upon it were, in truth, distractions. This is not to deny that the functioning of the labour market is of very great importance. If the labour market either transmits external cost pressures (as in 1974 in the UK) or if it generates them itself (as in 1968 in France and 1969 in Italy) this will make the operation of demand management far more difficult. Moreover, if inflationary pressures are very high and if society is unwilling or unable to reduce the growth of money wages through social consensus then a period of unemployment may well be the only alternative.

Nevertheless, none of these problems in the labour market removes Keynes' central insight that, if there is inadequate macroeconomic demand, there will be involuntary unemployment. Friedman's 1975 article simply ignores this possibility. In particular, with inadequate demand the labour market cannot clear no matter how flexible wages may be. Indeed, as Keynes pointed out on more than one occasion, there are circumstances in which a fall in wages will reduce demand and so exacerbate the problem rather than cure it.

The central problem is that neither the aggregate level of demand nor the stability of demand are guaranteed by decentralised markets. There has to be a coordinator.

The second lesson of the post-war period is that the coordination of aggregate demand has to have an international dimension. The 1950s and the 1960s worked well but this was simply luck. If the world economy is to work well in the future neither international demand management nor the financing of balance of payments flows can just be left to chance. Moreover, while coordination is undoubtedly difficult, it *is* possible to improve on recent experience.

In the cases of the recessions of both 1981 and 1991, policy was much much worse than it need have been.

The need to consider international coordination is especially pressing now. In the first part of 1994 the financial markets imposed a substantial tightening of monetary policy. In addition, even before this occurred, monetary policy (as measured by short-term real interest rates) was tighter than at the comparable stage of earlier economic cycles; and, unless there is a marked acceleration in inflation, the recent rise in medium term rates has put these back to near record levels in real terms. On top of this, many of the major countries are planning to tighten fiscal policy at the same time. As a result, the combination of tighter monetary and tighter fiscal policy poses a real threat to the possibly fragile recovery now under way. If in 1994 or 1995 the US economy were to slow or the recovery in Europe were to falter it would be imperative to relax fiscal policy.

The third lesson is the interaction between macroeconomic (demand) policies and microeconomic (supply) policies. What stands out in virtually all accounts of the Golden Age is the complementarity during this period of high levels of demand (which allowed and encouraged investment and labour mobility and structural change) with free trade, competition and rapid productivity growth.

The same argument, but unfortunately producing exactly opposite effects, applies to the 1980s and 1990s. Low levels of demand have discouraged investment and structural change. In addition, in the recessions of both 1981 and 1991 both physical and human capital has been scrapped. Unemployed workers have lost skills and, in some cases, the motivation to find new ones. As a result, what began as cyclical unemployment has turned into structural unemployment (this process is termed 'hysteresis' by economists because of the analogy with engineering in which the squeezing of a spring uses up energy so that the contraction and expansion paths are not identical). Moreover, many of the attempts at supply side reforms have been negated by the lack of demand. Part of any solution to structural unemployment must include training, but many people have become so cynical of obtaining a job that this policy has become like pushing water uphill. Overall, and most tellingly, productivity growth has declined.

Policy implications

The lessons from the past have some obvious implications for future policy. The most striking is that the way out of unemployment must be to use both demand side and supply side policies. Not only will neither on its own be sufficient, but also one without the other will produce adverse results. Demand management on its own will produce inflation; supply management on its own will produce unemployment.

As far as demand is concerned two moves are required. First, there needs to be a new institutional structure to arrange the coordination of policy; and second, the choice of policy needs to be appropriate.

The institutional structure should include at least the following. Coordination amongst the major industrialised countries should build on the existence of the G7 group. This should be reinforced by a permanent secretariat which might operate in much the same way as Working Party 3 of the OECD used to – monitoring the fiscal and monetary policies of individual countries and requiring these countries to give accounts of themselves. In addition, the European Council of Finance Ministers (ECOFIN) which includes representation by both Treasury and Central Banks should be similarly reinforced, focusing on coordination within Europe and on the determination of the exchange rate for the European Union as a whole.

In the case of policy, there should be an increase in international liquidity by further issues of Special Drawing Rights (and much of this liquidity should probably be used to help Eastern Europe finance its balance of payments difficulties). In addition, there should be a demand stimulus focused primarily on investment. Moreover, it should be investment with a wide range of benefits such as infrastructure, research and development expenditure or training. Since such spending has a wide set of externalities it should be public investment. In any case, it probably has to be primarily public investment because of the well-known difficulties of stimulating private investment (though temporary incentives to private investment focusing especially on bringing forward such investment should also be considered).

Another feature of any demand expansion is that it should be concentrated where unemployment is high. This implies focusing especially on long-term male unemployment. Construction projects and housing projects are therefore especially beneficial.

Given the concern about the debt levels in individual countries within Europe, this investment should largely be financed at the European level. There should, in effect, be a thirteenth borrower. As the Labour Party has suggested, there should be a European Recovery Programme which would borrow during slumps and repay during booms. Finally, the exact scale of any such fiscal stimulus to investment in the period immediately ahead must be judged in the light of the effects of the monetary and fiscal tightening that is already occurring. Any faltering in the European recovery would justify a particularly large scale programme.

An investment programme of this kind would have many advantages. Investment projects naturally come to an end so any increase in public expenditure would be temporary not permanent (thus at least part of the 'broomstick' problem would solve itself). Being carried out at the European level it would be independent of the political business cycle, and being both international and time-limited it would be more likely to pass the credibility test of the financial markets – and being investment it would add to supply as well as to demand.

One final point remains to be made. Much of the necessary action to reduce unemployment on the supply side is microeconomic, where the emphasis should be on correcting market failure. There is a great deal to be done here. However, I have emphasised macroeconomic policy both because the fashion has been to reject the usefulness of macro policy and, more importantly, because this is an essential accompaniment if supply side policies are to work. This is true both economically and politically. There should be an obligation on people to take work if it is available, but there can be no such obligation unless the Government plays a major part in ensuring that work *is* available. Obligation is a reciprocal relationship.

Many years ago Marshall likened demand and supply to a pair of scissors and commented that it was easy to fool oneself that only one blade was doing all the work. The same is true today of macro policy and micro policy. Both are essential.

References

[1]Maddison, A, *Phases of Capitalist Development,* OUP, 1982

[2]Matthews, RCO, *Why has Britain had Full Employment since the War?,* Economic Journal, Vol. 778 (1968), 555-569

[3]Friedman, M, *Unemployment versus Inflation?*, IEA Occasional Paper No. 44 (1975)

[4]Graham, AWM, *International Finance: The Need for a Residual Borrower,* International Financing of Economic Development: Proceedings of Second World Scientific Banking Meeting, May 26-31, 1980 (Remes, Beograd), 1982

[5]Allsopp, CJ, *The Assessment: Strategic Policy Dilemmas for the 1990s,* Oxford Review of Economic Policy, Vol. 9, No. 3 (1994)

Does America have the answer?

3

Jeff Faux

"Not too many years ago, the conventional wisdom was that Europe and Japan did it all right, and the US did it all wrong. And everything that could be learned, we could learn from them, and indeed, they had nothing to learn from us. Now the new conventional wisdom is just the opposite; we're doing everything right, and Europe and Japan are doing everything wrong. Neither of those positions is correct."

US Secretary of Labor, Robert Reich, commenting at the Detroit Jobs Conference, 14th March, 1994.

In the running, self-referencing dialogue among elites of most of the advanced nations, it is today's conventional wisdom that the United States offers the best model for competing in the new global economy. Some of the discussion reflects simple conservative bias. Some of it is a result of superficial and confused economic analysis. Nevertheless, this view is so widely accepted that social democrats must address it if the political debate is to move forward.

As commonly formulated, the argument follows that, compared with Europe, the US:

- *Created more jobs.* Thus, according to one recent commentary in *The Washington Post*: "The record is unmistakably clear. Since 1970 the US economy has generated 41 million new jobs; since the 1990-91 recession, the total is 3 million to 4 million (different surveys report different totals). By contrast, the European Union has created 8 million new jobs since 1970.

With a population nearly a third larger than ours, it has generated only 20% of the jobs. Its unemployment rate is 11%, up from 3% in 1970".

- *Lowered labour costs*. According to *The New York Times*, the US is now the "low-cost provider of many sophisticated products and services from plastics to software to financial services".

- *Restructured its firms, which are now expanding their world market shares*. As another article in *The New York Times* recently put it: "After more than a decade of painful change and dislocation, many American industries are leaner and nimbler, and others have seized the leadership of the sophisticated techhnologies that are ushering in the information age".

This sort of evidence is commonly offered as proof that the American Model – characterized by deregulation, weak unions and a minimalist welfare state – is the paradigm for surviving in the global economy, and that the sooner Europe accepts this, the better off it will be. Not surprisingly, this model was the pre-existing paradigm of choice of the policy, business, and media elites who frame the discussion.

This sweeping argument is not supported by the evidence.

Job creation

Inasmuch as those who point to the American Model are making the case for laissez-faire policies, the evidence must be drawn from the experience of the Reagan years forward, when deregulation took hold, business was encouraged to attack unions and the social safety net was shredded. Indeed, the previous decade of the 1970s was one in which the US welfare state was expanding. Adjusting for the effects of the business cycle, this means studying the closest peak-to-peak time frame – 1979-89.

As Larry Mishel and Jared Bernstein of the Economic Policy Institute have pointed out, an examination of job and economic growth during that period leaves one less than breathless about the American Model. Table 1, reflecting their calculations, shows that US per capita GDP growth averaged 1.5% from 1979-89, compared with 2.3% for eight other nations for which comparable data are available. Moreover, when the data are decomposed to show the share of growth resulting from a change in the employment/population ratio compared with a change in productivity, it turns out that the share of US growth attributable to productivity was the lowest of any of the other nations, save one. Thus, US growth in the 1980s relied less on a healthy rise in economic efficiency than an increase in the proportion of its population that chose, or was forced, to go to work.

Table 1

Contributions to per capita GDP growth in nine countries, 1979-89

	Annual Growth Rate (GDP per Capita)	Percent of Growth Due to:	
		Emp/Pop %	Productivity %
Canada	2.0	41	59
Japan	3.3	16	84
France	1.7	-28	128
Germany	1.6	18	82
Italy	2.2	10	90
Netherlands	1.0	60	40
Sweden	1.8	28	72
UK	2.1	18	82
US	1.5	51	49
Non-US weighted average (by population, averaging the endpoints)	2.3	13	87

(Source: EPI, Mishel & Bernstein analysis of US Bureau of Labor Statistics data, 1994

Table 2 shows that US job growth during the 1980s was high relative to other nations – although lower than that of Canada and Australia, which are in general more regulated, have higher rates of unionization and have more generous welfare states. What all three countries have in common are high rates of population growth – especially from immigration. Obviously, slow population growth and, therefore, slow labour force growth, is a constraint on the capacity of an economy to generate jobs. Accordingly, Table 2 shows that population increase was the major contributor to the growth of jobs in those high employment nations during the 1980s. The growth of jobs relative to the population in the US was, of course, respectable, but hardly spectacular. And it certainly does not justify the conclusion that the American economy is uniquely structured for job creation.

Alone among the advanced nations, real wages of production workers in the US fell from 1979 to 1989 (Table 3). As Bill Clinton said during the 1992 campaign, Americans were working "harder for less". At the same time, of course, we had the Reagan/Bush deficits, which were clearly a major engine of job growth through the decade. Thus, in order to achieve the growth in jobs that it did, the US had to lower living standards for the majority of its people and quadruple its debt. It is hard to find in this record support for the simple-minded notion, constantly repeated and amplified by politicians and the press, that the deregulated US economy outperformed the rest of the industrial nations and should therefore be the exemplar of economic policy for the coming decade.

Table 2
Contributions to employment growth in ten countries, 1973-92 (annual rates of change)

| | Growth contribution of: | | |
	Employment growth	Population %	Emp/Pop %
1973-79			
UK	0.22	0.01	0.22
France	0.36	0.47	-0.11
Germany	-0.57	-0.17	-0.40
Italy	0.91	0.45	0.46
Japan	0.67	1.07	-0.40
Canada	2.85	1.23	1.62
Australia	0.97	1.20	-0.23
Netherlands	2.63	0.73	1.90
Sweden	1.25	0.32	0.93
US	2.50	1.00	1.50
Non-US weighted average	0.60	0.50	0.10
(by population, averaging the endpoints)			
1979-89			
UK	0.57	0.18	0.39
France	0.07	0.51	-0.44
Germany	0.64	0.11	0.53
Italy	0.41	0.22	0.20
Japan	1.13	0.61	0.52
Canada	1.83	0.99	0.84
Australia	2.35	1.46	0.88
Netherlands	1.26	0.56	0.70
Sweden	0.84	0.24	0.60
US	1.72	1.00	0.72
Non-US weighted average	0.83	0.45	0.37
(by population, averaging the endpoints)			

(Source: EPI, Mishel & Bernstein analysis of US Bureau of Labor Statistics, 1994)

Moreover, as Table 2 also indicates, over the previous business cycle of the 1970s, when the US welfare state was at its most expansive, American job growth was even better vis-a-vis Europe than during the cycle of the 1980s.

After 1989, the US economy turned downward. During the next three years, real wages for production workers continued to decline. Deficits in 1990, 1991, and 1992 rose to 4.0, 4.8, and 4.9% of GDP, respectively. Inasmuch as employ-

Table 3
Hourly manufacturing compensation growth, 1979-89

Country	All Employees %	Produduction Workers
Canada	0.4	0.5
Denmark	-0.1	0.3
France	1.7	2.1
West Germany	2.4	1.8
Italy	0.9	0.6
Japan	1.8	1.3
Netherlands	0.8	0.9
Sweden	0.5	0.9
United Kingdom	2.0	1.7
United States	0.2	-0.6

(Source: EPI, Mishel & Bernstein analysis of US Bureau of Labor statistics data, 1994)

ment was stagnant over the long recession in the US, job growth during this period certainly does not provide much evidence to support the superiority of the American Model. This brings us down to the single year 1993 – the remaining year left for making the case. The federal deficit was reduced, interest rates fell and the government contribution to the economy shrunk. Even in 1993, however, the first two quarters of the year were quite sluggish, GDP growing at 0.8 and 1.9%.

This narrows the case down to the last two quarters of 1993, in which growth accelerated smartly. This was certainly a good performance but not one that was out of line with previous recoveries. In fact, if current job growth was as robust as the average for previous recoveries, the US would have another three or four million jobs.

Thus, the celebrated case for the American Model rests primarily on the evidence of two quarters of growth in an otherwise anaemic recover.

Shrinking real earnings

The press often treats the downward pressure on living standards as if it were a mysterious phenomenon independent of the improved 'competitiveness' of US business, but few serious advocates of the American Model would deny that lower labour costs at this point are reflected in economic and social pain among people who work for a living. Nor is there much doubt that lower levels of real wages and benefits, drastic corporate downsizing and jobs-shedding and a dozen years of efforts to undercut labour unions have been the major causes.

The pattern is by now familiar. The decline of real wages has put the squeeze on family incomes, accelerating the entry of married women into the work force and the rise of the number of people working more than one job. There has been an expansion of temporary and contingent jobs as employers shed the more expensive full-time workers, both reducing the cost of fringe benefits and creating workplaces harder for unions to organize. At the same time, those who do have full time jobs have seen their work day stretched out. Hours of work are rising. Among workers in non-union firms, it is not uncommon for much of this "overtime" to be off the clock and therefore unpaid. In the lower and middle reaches of the white-collar world, many American workers report that the 50-hour week has become a standard.

Less familiar is the breadth of the earnings deterioration. The greatest losses are of course being experienced by the less educated, the younger, the non-whites, and the males. (Women's real hourly wages for those at the median level or above grew during the 1980s but from a much lower base, and the 'gender gap' between men's and women's wages remains substantial.) But the tide of job stress has been rising up the educational pyramid; since 1987, real hourly earnings of male US college graduates have been falling.

Corporate downsizing has, of course, hit both blue- and white-collar America with a vengeance. Even amidst the overall growth of the last half of 1993, US newspapers were full of grim news of massive layoffs in firms that had also previously experienced job shedding. Indeed, there is evidence that firing workers and forcing those who are left to work harder does not solve most firms' problems. Recent studies have shown that a majority of US corporate downsizings did not accomplish the efficiency and profitability objectives that motivated them. For example, business school professor Kim Cameron of the University of Michigan found that of 150 companies that had downsized, 75% ended up worse off.

Benign restructuring?

Those who promote the American Model sometimes argue that we should not expect the deregulation of the American economy of the late 1970s and early 1980s to show up in time to be adequately measured over the business cycle of the 1980s. So they frequently cite the relative reduction in US labour costs in manufacturing that occurred from the mid-1980s as a proxy for improved US competitiveness. Typically, this is presented in terms of US dollars, since in the actual marketplace, competitive advantage includes the effects of currency fluctuations. But the improved performance resulting from the drop in the US dollar during the last half of the 1980s is hardly a measure of returning economic strength.

As Table 4 shows, the performance of the American Model looks much more modest when the effect of the changing value of the dollar is separated out.

Table 4
Unit labour costs in manufacturing, 1985-92
(annual percentage change)

Country	National Currency %	US Dollars %
Belgium	1.5	10.7
Canada	4.0	5.8
Denmark	3.9	12.6
France	1.3	9.3
Germany	3.3	13.1
Italy	4.4	11.1
Japan	1.2	10.8
Netherlands	1.4	11.0
Norway	4.7	9.7
Sweden	5.0	11.0
United Kingdom	8.5	8.6
United States	1.3	1.3

(Source: US Bureau of Labor Statistics, Monthly Labor Review, December 1993, pg.52)

Overall US business productivity actually decelerated after 1985, averaging less than 1% per year through 1991. In 1992, productivity rose 3.3% but then became negative in the first two quarters of 1993. Again, as with the job growth argument, this rests the productivity case for the American Model on the narrow evidence of its performance in the second six months of 1993.

Inasmuch as the numbers are unconvincing, many enthusiasts of the American Model cite anecdotal evidence: the reversal of fortune of some US firms who now claim to be expanding their market shares, not simply on the basis of lower labour costs but by virtue of having 're-invented' the corporation. According to this argument, US management, unfettered by union rules and social restraints, has reengineered its firms to make them more efficient and better able to cope with the accelerated pace of change and intense competition of the new global marketplace.

Much of this claim is overblown, filled with the self-congratulatory hot air that diffuses through the pages of business magazines to comfort a readership anxious to be reassured that its profits represent a giving, not a taking, from society. The vast majority of US firms that have 'come back' are doing so by squeezing wages, outsourcing to Mexico and other Third World countries and forcing longer hours on their workers. There is no need for fancy explanations to understand what is going on in most of them.

Having said that, there is some evidence of a movement to restructure US firms in a way that may be more benign. In fact, notwithstanding the romanticism and dangers of employee manipulation that may be involved, it could be argued that these efforts can lead to production systems that empower workers and enhance job satisfaction. It could be argued further that the greater flexibility of American managers has enabled them to move faster in this direction than managers in Europe. Eileen Appelbaum of EPI has surveyed so-called high-performance workplaces in a number of US firms and has identified cases where genuine downward redistribution of power and authority has taken place as a result of management initiatives in both union and non-union settings.

But as she has also discovered, other elements in the American Model work against this kind of transformation of the workplace. One element is the tyranny of the financial markets that force short-term horizons on production firms. Firms are judged today by Wall Street investors not on the basis of the improved worker-management relations that a high-performance workplace requires but according to the ruthlessness with which they treat their labour, which is taken as evidence of a management's dedication to efficiency. Indeed, some US firms that were a short time ago regarded as pioneers in their efforts to create empowering workplaces in partnership with unions have in recent months reversed themselves, despite hard evidence of success, because the stock market was taking a dim view of it.

Appelbaum has also found that the transformation of the workplace requires a large up-front investment in training that most American firms are unwilling to pay. In the US, training employed workers is seen almost exclusively as a private sector matter and therefore little public funds are available to defray the costs. During his campaign, President Clinton proposed a French-style programme in which a small payroll tax would be levied on corporations and then forgiven to the extent that the firms establish a qualified programme. But the proposal has been shelved because of opposition from business.

Another characteristic that makes the American Model hostile toward the transformation of the workplace is the much greater mobility of the US labour force. This raises the risk that firms who do make the investment in training their workers will see them captured by other firms who can afford to pay higher wages precisely because they have not accepted the costs of training. A low-wage, contingent-work labour market discourages loyalty to the firm even more.

The 'Clinton model'

The good news is that the Clinton Administration is trying to move America away from some of the worst aspects of the American Model as commonly defined: mindless deregulation, hostility toward unions and minimalist government. In some sense, the Administration is trying to deal with the failure of the Reagan/Bush policies with a minimum challenge to business ideology.

For starters, unlike his immediate predecessors, the President and most of his economic advisors acknowledge the basic principles of macroeconomics. In fact, they came into office proposing a fiscal stimulus. For a variety of reasons, the effort failed in the Congress. So Clinton shifted to a 'second-best' monetary stimulus. The White House agreed to spending cuts and tax increases to reduce the deficit on the understanding that the Federal Reserve Board would accommodate lower long-term interest rates. The Treasury Department helped by shifting its financing of the deficit away from long-term bonds, which raised their prices and lowered their yields. (Some observers believe that it was this so-called 'operation twist' as much or more than the reduced deficit projections that influenced long-term rates.)

The policy was successful, generating good growth in the second half of 1993 that was led by interest-sensitive industries such as housing and consumer durables. But there are already clouds on the horizon. With the official unemployment rate still well above 6%, the Federal Reserve raised short-term interest rates in February. The President was assured by the economics establishment, for whom Fed Chair Alan Greenspan can do no wrong, that this would have no effect on long-term rates. Sage heads nodded that long-term rates would be benefit because the bond markets would be reassured that the Fed remained vigilant against inflation. But as the sceptics feared, long-term rates shot up and are now above where they were a year ago. No one knows at this point how much this will cut into US economic growth but it is obvious that the Administration's only available macroeconomic policy lever has been, for the moment, rendered rather impotent. Perhaps more important, the Federal Reserve has put us on notice that it has no intention of allowing the economy to reach full employment.

There is also good news in the Clinton government's open acknowledgement that the government has a responsibility for reducing structural unemployment. The Administration has initiated the beginnings of a civilian industrial policy, which includes more support for research and development and discussions with specific industries on ways in which the government can speed up getting new ideas to market. It is also setting up regional industrial 'extension services' for the diffusion of technology to small- and medium-sized businesses – an approach inspired by the agricultural extension services that were a major factor in expanding agricultural productivity in the US a half century ago.

On the human capital side, Secretary of Labor, Robert Reich, has been given a modest budget increase to expand and reorganize the federal government's training and labour market services. Extra help will go to dislocated older workers and a welcome expansion of vocational programs aimed at young people who do not go on to college. And there are the stirrings in Reich's Department of the first serious effort by the federal government to nurture programmes of worker empowerment at the job site.

The bad news is that these efforts are too small scale, in both size and conception, to deal with the problems of structural unemployment – particularly given the Administration's other strategic initiatives that could well make the problems worse.

Reflected in its policies toward NAFTA and GATT, the Clinton Administration has thus far accepted the Bush assumption that future US economic growth depends on an expanding export market. Indeed, a consistent theme of Clinton's is that the core problem of the US economy lies in workers not being willing to "embrace" world competition and technological change.

It is obvious that there are some big questions here. One is the wisdom of giving priority to an export sector, which accounts for less than 10% of the economy, over the domestic sector, which accounts for over 90%. Another is the tendency of the Administration to ignore the fact that globalization means rising imports as well as exports. Export-led growth is also the dream of most of the other 100-plus signatories to GATT. The large US trade deficit casts not a small shadow on the assumption that American industry has become so competitive that it can overcome the growing propensity of the economy to import. Some 20 to 25% of the increment to US national income now leaks out in the form of imports. These and other questions have largely been shoved aside by a romantic commercial boosterism in which unspecified assertions about vast consumer markets overseas panting for US goods and services are taken as facts.

Sensible people can, of course, have different views of the export-led growth strategy. But even if one accepts its premises, it is clear that the Administration's budgetary commitment to the adjustment and public investment programs falls short of the minimum that is needed to support its trade expansion agenda. Instead of investing more in human and physical infrastructure, the Administration and Congress have agreed to a five-year budget plan that will leave the US even further behind; the share of US GDP devoted to domestic public investments will actually decline. Moreover, many of Clinton's policies will make economic life more precarious for those at the bottom of the workforce. Even free traders admit that NAFTA and the lowering of trade barriers against Third World countries will shrink job opportunities for low-wage workers. A proposal to limit welfare to two years could dump another two million people on to the low-wage labour market. And health care reform will slow job growth in the one industry that has seen expanding opportunities for minorities and the less educated. The immediate outlook is for more job stress at the bottom without the promised compensatory programs.Having lost to congressional deficit hawks last year, and being unwilling to force more cuts on the military, Clinton does not have the money for the investments his strategy requires. All he has left is the 'cut and spend' tactic of chipping away small sums from some domestic programs to shift to others, and yet another variant of the hoary proposition that bringing business methods to government will somehow convince voters that the public sector will become more efficient, and therefore more loved. Some of this reprioritizing and reorganization makes sense (although after 12 years of Reagan and Bush there is not a great deal of fat left in the domestic budget) but the savings will be small. Besides, since many of these programs are hotly defended, this requires the President to become embroiled in large battles with Congress that cannot, in any case, free up the resources he needs.

Bill Clinton's sentiments toward working people and the poor are clearly warmer than were those of Reagan or Bush. And it is a relief to have people in government with good ideas for reform and expansion of social programmes, and who come out of a dozen years of experimenting at the state and community level. America is, in fact, full of examples of projects that have worked and people who know how to run them. But the money is too scarce for much more than modest small-scale activities. At best, this is so far a 'pilot programme presidency'. And it raises the question of just how much difference it will make in the end. The distinction between a government that doesn't care and a government that cares but cannot find the money to provide much help, is likely to be lost on the worker whose financial life, and personal life as well, may be in tatters as a result of the government's eagerness to embrace the global marketplace.

Beyond pain allocation

Both the so-called American Model of low wages and high employment and the so- called European Model of high wages and low employment are, in effect, models of how to allocate the pain – the pain of adjustment to the new brutally competitive global economy. The assumption that there is a 'trade-off' between them is based on the notion that free trade and deregulation will unleash market forces that will somehow find a prosperous equilibrium. Thus, it is said, if we take the punishment now, squeeze out 'excessive' wages and benefits, liquidate debt and reduce the burden of social welfare, our companies will become leaner and meaner, move ahead of other nations and, at some point in the future, enlarge market share and restore prosperity. This is neo-liberal folly at its most destructive.

None of those who confidently jabber on about the long-term benefits of short-term pain can answer the critical question: *How long will it take?* For example, economic theory, as well as common sense, tells us that when low-wage and high-wage workers are thrown into competition in the same markets with similar capital equipment, their wages will tend to converge. But the gaps are so large that the process extends far beyond the practical time horizon of economic policy. To give one example: if Mexican real wages were to grow at 4% per year and US wages were to stagnate, it would take almost 50 years for them to equalize and, presumably, at that point for both to begin to rise together.

29

The circumstances are quite different, of course, but the current conventional wisdom is eerily reminiscent of the economic discourse that dominated the 1930s – the last long period of high unemployment. The stubborn insistence on balancing public budgets in the face of large-scale unemployment was justified by the argument that the world had to rely on market forces to 'restructure' its way out of the Depression. One prominent economist expressed the consensus in 1932 when he wrote: "We shall come out of it only through hard work and readjustments that are painful. There is no other alternative".

But of course, the world did not wait for market-driven restructuring. Before the forces of supply and demand could drive incomes and prices low enough to spark a satisfactory revival of investment, the political reaction to economic pain set in motion the most destructive war in history. As we all know, the unemployment problems of the 1930s were solved not by market forces but by government spending that was the exact opposite of the tight fiscal strategy advocated by the economic policy intellectuals of the time.

The question that seems to drive the internal economic debates in most of the advanced nations is: *How do we compete in this new global economy?* But the verb 'to compete' lends itself to many interpretations. For example, balanced trade can be achieved with high levels of unemployment. Market share in individual industries can be maintained by constantly lowering wages. And a nation can often compensate for the unattractiveness of its goods by permitting its currency value to sink lower and lower. Moreover, although international trade volumes are growing more rapidly than output, the great bulk of what most advanced industrial nations produce is still for their own domestic market. Only 7% of the GDP of the OECD countries in Europe is represented by imports, only 8% of Japan's GDP, and just 11% of the US'.

A better question is: *How do we achieve full employment with rising real incomes?*

The difference between the two questions is critical. If the primary goal is to compete, then, for example, European labour market systems, which support higher wages and a shorter work week, will be seen as an obstacle to the priority goal of reducing labour costs. But if the point is to raise incomes, such systems may well be necessary. It is not clear that the US model in which family incomes must be maintained by more people working and working longer hours, makes a superior contribution to human happiness and social stability than does a European economic model in which family incomes are maintained by fewer people working less.

Indeed, it is largely a waste of time to continue pondering the so-called 'trade-offs' between high-unemployment/high-wage strategies and low-unemployment/low-wage strategies. The more important issue is how to create an international economic environment that can support a high-wage path to accelerated job creation, which would give individuals the freedom to make trade-offs between hours of work and leisure.

Implicit in this issue is the idea that the advanced industrial nations not only have problems in common but that their solutions to some extent must be collective. Given the growing competitive environment, there is a limit to the ability of any one nation – even one as large as the United States of America – to implement policies to raise living standards at home unless other nations are taking similar steps. The challenge is to move from 'beggar-thy-neighbour' policies, in which living standards are progressively sacrificed to the goal of competitiveness, to a cooperative effort in which competition takes place in such a way that raises standards everywhere.

This was clearly one of the motivating factors that led Bill Clinton to call the G-7 jobs conference in Detroit in March 1994. Yes, as in any event, there were political motivations. Nevertheless, there are at least some people in this Administration who recognize that there is only so far even the US can go on its present course unless it can work out an answer to the question: *How will the global economy be managed?*

The neo-liberal answer is to leave it to the market. But that answer was rejected after the 1930s because it didn't work. And only the hopelessly naive can believe that the post World War II era could have avoided the fate that befell us after World War I without a strong government hand to regulate our national economies and a strong United States to regulate the global one.

We all know that that era is now over and that if we are successfully to move to a new one it will require a Bretton Woods II. Indeed, if we are lucky, the Detroit conference, with all of its disappointments and disgruntlements, may turn out some day to have represented another step in the slouching of the rough G-7 beast towards that economic Bethlehem.

Thus, it would be a serious mistake for social democrats elsewhere to look at the Clinton Administration only in terms of some clever national or local policy ideas that can solve their jobs problems. By all means let us share ideas and information. But no one should forget that the US is still one of the most conservative of the advanced nations and the experience just discussed should make it clear that it has no magic policy bullet.

Indeed, one message of the Clinton experience so far is that social democrats all over need to begin serious work on developing an alternative to the international neo-liberal paradigm. For example, we need to make more credible the possibilities of simultaneous expansionary fiscal and monetary policy, the development of the Third World along progressive lines, the strengthening of the social contract – labour, human, and environmental rights – in and among all nations, and disabuse our fellow citizens of the idea that only economic austerity can protect them from inflation.

No doubt many will view the idea of collective economic policy as utopian. The G-7 can hardly bring itself to agree on the bland wording of the inconsequential joint statements that burp out at the end of their periodic summits. How can we ever expect anything more?

The answer is that we can't – without the transformation of politics in these nations that should be our underlying purpose. And one piece in the overall mosaic of a transformed politics is for the mainstream Left to challenge the neo-liberal ideological hegemony over the discussion of international relationships in a global economy. Otherwise, labour and social democrats will continue to be boxed in by those who carry the political water for multinational corporations and who have become exceedingly creative in depicting us as protectionists, defenders of the obsolete and obstacles to the hi-tech miracles that corporations can perform if only we unfetter them from tiresome rules and nationalist conceits.

International cooperation is not a substitute for national economic policies and the politics that go with them. It cannot come about unless we elect governments who want to create jobs and rising living standards and see that they are restrained by an increasingly unstable global marketplace. But if we are becoming part of a 'global economy' (and I believe we are, although the phrase does not capture all of economic reality) then in order to be politically useful we must offer a credible vision of international economic cooperation. Otherwise, we cannot explain how we will break out of the trap in which present and future domocratic governments do and will find themselves.

The people may actually be ahead of us all. Certainly, there is in America much acknowledged scepticism about the claims made for the American Model. In a recent article on low-wage jobs, *The New York Times* interviewed a husband and wife who had two jobs apiece that earned them a total of $18,000 last year. When told by the reporter that the booming US economy was now generating jobs at the rate of almost two million a year, the husband responded: "Sure, we've got four of them. So what?".

Where the macro meets the structural

4

Robert Kuttner

The world economic system is now characterised by globalised markets, worldwide rationalisation of production, shedding of excess labour and increasing pressure on firms and nations to compete. According to neo-classical economics, our economies should therefore be experiencing heroic increases in productivity and growth. But despite – or more likely because of – its new openness, the global economy of the 1990s is persistently sluggish. And because of the increased marketisation, the fruits of productivity growth are distributed with rising inequality.

Domestically, rising innovation and productivity growth are occurring in a macro-economic context of high unemployment, rationalisation and redundancy. This means that technical progress which should be a blessing for the economy as a whole is a curse for individual workers. That alone tells us that the conventional structural remedies will not solve the problem.

Much of what we read insists the solution to slow growth and joblessness is more of the same – a redoubling of efforts to secure greater marketisation and fiscal prudence: end the remnants of communism in the east and statism in the west, cut public sector deficits, privatise and deregulate, raise savings rates to reduce capital costs, connect the poor nations of the south to the global marketplace, let competitive pressure steer resources to optimal uses – and our economies will soar.

This view is startlingly pre-Keynesian. It ignores the fact that while globalisation and hyper-marketisation may increase the feverishness of competition, these trends also undercut the very stabilisers that undergirded the Bretton Woods era of high and broadly diffused growth. The elements of that system included not just fixed exchange rates and macro-economic management country by country, but also national regulatory and wage-setting institutions and national industrial development strategies that taken together defined the paradigmatic post-War mixed economy. Nonetheless, the conventional prescription undergirds the thinking of *bien pensants* throughout the west and informs virtually all major recent policy initiatives – the Uruguay Round of the GATT, the NAFTA agreement, the cold-bath approach to the reconstruction of the former Soviet bloc and the ubiquitous privatisation and deregulation efforts throughout the OECD and the developing world.

A national world

In the aftermath of World War II, a mixed economy was attainable at the level of the nation-state because the nation-state controlled its borders. That made it possible for nations to have national fiscal, monetary, regulatory, social, sectoral and developmental policies. These included macro-economic management; social contracts between industry and labour predicated on non-inflationary full employment; economic development strategies that used subsidy, preferential procurement, and technology-forcing via regulation; tight supervision and the regulation of financial institutions both to stabilise those instutions, to facilitate monetary policy, and to use banks as engines of national development. The United States, as the dominant economy and keeper of the peace, helped stimulate global recovery both by exporting capital, by serving as the residual market for other nations' products exports, and by serving as architect and guarantor of the Bretton Woods/GATT framework.

In addition, large, stable mass-production firms in basic industry and collective bargaining with labour unions created an industrial context that stabilised wages. The result was a virtuous circle at the national level, of rising productivity, which translated into rising real wages, which enabled mass consumption of the economic product. This, in turn, created increasing opportunities for investment, which kept the productivity increases coming. This virtuous economic system allowed a companion virtuous political circle. Centre-Left parties as champions of a mixed economy could be the custodians of its social contract. A stable production system of rising growth and a broadly diffused living system created and reinforced solidarities and conferred legitimacy on the system's architects. Even Centre-Right parties, especially Catholic ones, were committed to economic security and social solidarity rather than hyper-marketisation. Trade unions were able to deliver real benefits with a clear role in advancing the welfare state and the economic standing of workers, allowing them effectively to mobilise constituencies for Centre-Left parties.

New world

By contrast, in the new economy nothing stays put very long. Nations have lost their macro-economic leverage because capital markets are now global. If a nation runs a macro-economic policy more expansive than its neighbours, the stimulus will only leak out into imports, producing price inflation and debasement of the national currency. Labour has lost the power to bargain for high wages because labour markets are increasingly worldwide, too. Wage-workers in poor nations lack the purchasing power to buy what they make, which means that global supply outruns global demand. Governments today are hesitant to regulate since capital moves to areas of lower regulation.

Despite the conventional view, evidence is accumulating that further global marketisation plus domestic deflation is not the solution to slow growth and falling wages. To a substantial degree, it is the problem. The global economy is in trouble today not because of the remaining barriers to free commerce but because their haphazard elimination has deprived economies and states of necessary stabilisers and energisers.

Among our governments, there is the beginning of a willingness to address structural questions, but it is tentative, timid and partly misplaced. At the March 1994 G-7 Detroit conference on jobs (downgraded from a promised jobs 'summit'), national leaders emphasized a combination of increased labour market "flexibility" plus enhanced investment in human capital, both to create jobs and to raise wages. This strategy is, to put it charitably, necessary but woefully insufficient.

The three efficiencies

The standard analysis emphasizes only one kind of economic efficiency – the static, allocative kind. By steering resources to their optimal uses and taking advantage of specialisation, we supposedly optimise growth. This view, which we might call Smithian efficiency, is still what dominates standard economics, six decades after Keynes.

However, it ignores two other brands of efficiency. Let us call them 'Keynesian Efficiency', and 'Schumpeterian Efficiency'. Keynesian Efficiency hardly needs elaborating. If the economy is performing well below its full-employment potential, it gets stuck in a high-unemployment equilibrium. Increasing allocative efficiency in such circumstances doesn't help. It may even hurt, to the extent that liberalised trade in a slow-growth era costs high-wage economies good jobs and hence purchasing power.

Accelerated competition in a low growth macro-economic context also causes relentless restructuring, wage-cutting and layoffs. Thus, the economy of the 1990s offers the terrible paradox of escalating gains to productivity via Smithian efficiency – coexisting with declining purchasing power and declining job security for most ordinary people.

By contrast, the experience of World War II for the domestic US economy is an epic case of an event that grossly violated allocative efficiency with wage and price controls, monopolistic military contracts and massive state intervention – yet stimulated Keynesian efficiency and quickly restored full employment. Despite a record debt/GDP ratio of 119.8% at the war's end – more than double the current 'dangerous' ratio – this high debt was perfectly compatible with two decades of record growth.

Standard economics does not know how to treat these two very different kinds of efficiency in the same analytical frame. As the Nobel laureate James Tobin once quipped, it takes a lot of Harberger triangles to fill up an Okun gap. Tobin's point was that that little allocative efficiencies – Professor Harberger's triangles – do not compensate for big, Keynesian inefficiencies of low growth, high unemployment and idle capacity. At the same time, his deliberately and splendidly mixed metaphor – triangles and gaps – also underscores that standard analysis lacks a common metric for assessing the interaction of these two conceptions of efficiency in the same conversation.

The postwar boom was also built on Schumpertian efficiencies. Schumpeter was the prophet of technical progress as the engine of growth and the defender of imperfect competition as the necessary agent of technical progress. Large, oligopolistic firms often turn out to have the deepest pockets and they keep innovating to defend their privileged market position and to fend off encroachment. Innovation within a structure of stable oligopoly may be more reliable than innovation in a context of fierce and mutually ruinous price competition. Casual readers (or non-readers) of Schumpeter may remember him as a prophet of "creative destruction" but this cartoon of Schumpeter has it backwards. Schumpeter's concern was how a market system could endure its propensities towards ruinous competition. He was no advocate of creative destruction.

As a matter of technical economics, there is a Schumpeter/Smith disjuncture as potent as the Keynes/Smith disjuncture. An economy that is performing according to the precepts of allocative efficiency is likely to have avoidable unemployment; it is also likely to produce under-investment in technological advance because of well known positive externality dilemmas: society underinvests in innovation. Indeed, the more 'perfect' the competition, the less money is left over to invest in innovations that have broadly diffused benefits but that may not pay off to the investor for decades, if ever. The greater the rate of creative destruction, the less available are the monopoly rents that are the innovator's reward and necessary shelter. The more the economy relies on casino-like capital markets and the less it relies on stable firms with long-term perspectives, the shorter the time horizons of investors and the less the availability of patient capital. When is oligopoly actually 'efficient?' From a Smithian perspective, the question is nonsensical *ex hypothesis*. From a Schumpeterian perspective, it is a matter of getting down to cases.

James Kurth, a political economist at Swarthmore College, has coined the useful phrase, "Military Schumpeterianism". This is an ingenious twist on the oft-repeated insight that the postwar boom was built on "Military Keynesianism". By Military Keynesianism one had in mind the reliable stimulus of defense spending, which substituted for a more explicit and aggressive Keynesianism of larger deficits for civilian purposes, socialised savings, public infrastructure investment and so on. Kurth's point is that while large and persistent military outlays may have had macroeconomic benefits, defense contracts also had immense benefits to innovation, stabilisation, and market leadership – they helped underpin Galbraith's New Industrial State. In a nation where the prevailing ideology rendered economic planning and public ownership largely illegitimate, the Pentagon was both MITI and Keynes.

A series of long term military contracts to a prime vendor produces assaults against allocative efficiency – Vice President Gore's famous cases of hundred dollar hammers, thousand dollar toilet seats, cost-plus windfalls – yet also produces stunning technical advances and market leadership. Who thinks that Boeing would be the world's leader in aircraft sales without WWII and the Cold War? As with Tobin's quip about triangles and gaps, standard economics has difficulty weighing the allocative loss of the hundred dollar hammer against the dynamic gain of jetliners.

Recent research by Maryellen R. Kelley of Carnegie-Mellon University suggests that in the US the network of military prime contractors and subcontractors also provide immense benefits in technical diffusion of best-practice manufacturing (which was necessary to meet difficult specifications and fine tolerances), analogous to similar benefits of Japanese keiretsu and German bank-industry-labour interlocks. The common element is long-term association and forms of competitive discipline offering shelter from pure price competition.

Structurally, the economy of the post-War boom (1948-73) lent itself to non-Smithian kinds of efficiency – and to steady growth. The market economies of that era were national, were sheltered from pure marketisation and were hence more amenable to management. The global economic rules of that era – fixed exchange rates, capital controls and managed trade – allowed entrepreneurship to flourish but limited its global dimension and tempered the rate of creative destruction.

Reinventing a mixed economy

The end of the Cold War, far from creating a peace dividend, has deprived our economies of public spending on research, technology, and infrastructure once carried out under military auspices. The neo-liberal GATT ethic deprives us of development subsidies carried out for more explicitly civilian or national purposes. Nor have we found a set of stabilising and dynamising institutions to provide either the respite from pure laissez-faire trade and finance offered by Bretton Woods; or the pseudo Keynesian demand managements benefits of

American military hegemony; or the labour-setting benefits of relatively trade-insulated national economies; or the Schumpeterian benefits of large oligopolies, regulated or nationalised industries and military contracts.

Indeed, the explicit policy goal of this era is to dismantle the remnants of that earlier, presumably wrongheaded system, not to replicate it. How odd that the imperfect competition of the 'forties, 'fifties and 'sixties produced 4% growth – and the creative destruction of the 'eighties and 'nineties is struggling to sustain 2%!

What to do?

By the midpoint of this decade, we may well see progressive governments back in power in Stockholm, London and Berlin and perhaps elsewhere. Should that happy event occur, do we really know what grand strategy and what national policies we wish them to pursue? How shall we restore the virtuous circle of the post-War boom? How shall we make sure that rising productivity again translates into rising real living standards, broadly diffused?

Are the main problems macro or structural? Is our task to reclaim some functional equivalent of the post-War system, in order to allow national economic management? Or has the world economy moved irrevocably beyond that stage? Must we recover the conditions for policies of stabilisation and full employment at the national level or the level of regional economic unions or globally? Is it practical to think of global regimes for credit-creation, macroeconomic policy, financial regulation, labour standards and conditional free trade? What sort of politics could undergird these policies and which version of the policies would have positive political feedback?

Structural or macro?

In the stylised debate between the structuralists and the macro-economists, there are progressive and reactionary constructions of the problem on both sides. For example, there are 'structuralists' who think the structural problem is welfare state rigidities and inadequately trained workers. Global marketisation has given new legitimacy to the claim that income distribution necessarily reflects merit and that the simple cure for low pay is better trained workers. If you lose your job, you should go out and become an entrepreneur. If Steven Jobs, the founder of Apple Computers, could start a billion dollar high-technology enterprise in his garage, so can you. And if you can't, it must be that you aren't as smart as Steven Jobs.

In this view, which pervades the thinking of the Clinton administration, most of the problem is one of human capital. The companion neo-liberal view holds that labour market rigidities are the essence of the problem. Make it easier to get rid of redundant workers, force firms to become more efficient and productivity will rise, unemployment will fall, and workers will eventually be paid what the market deems they 'deserve'.

The orthodox macroeconomic view, companion to the orthodox structural view, holds that the macro problem is too much public borrowing: real interest rates may be too high, but that this is the result of a bloated public sector. In this view, greater fiscal balance will bring the rewards of lower interest rates and higher growth.

However, the American evidence is that the weakening of wage-setting institutions and social contracts and the increase in Smithian effieciency at the firm level does not produce either enough jobs or enough good jobs, especially in a context of high macroeconomic unemployment. A better version of Smith doesn't get you to Keynes. Moreover, in the context of globalisation and deregulation, rising productivity does not necessarily translate into rising living standards, especially for those in competition with the global reserve army. For example, the productivity of US autoworkers, textile workers or steelworkers rose dramatically during the 1980s yet their real wages fell by 10-20%. The productivity of routine workers who use computers – insurance clerks, bank tellers, checkout clerks and such like rose sharply as well and their wages were flat. In Europe, where wages tended to keep pace with productivity; instead of sharing wage cuts, more workers lost their jobs. But the underlying dynamic was the same. Rising productivy did not produce rising economic gains for ordinary people.

Therefore, even if we concede the desirability of a better educated and trained workforce, even if we grant the virtue of Clinton-Delors-style "positive flexibility" (retraining and re-employment rather than the dole), we should recognise that human capital policies do not by themselves solve the macroeconomic problem. Indeed, the Clinton-Delors approach thus far is an underfunded and under-analysed version of what Swedish Keynesians did invented in the 1950s with far more ideological clarity about its logic and purpose.

Beyond better trained workers, our economies require a renewed commitment to full employment borh for for its own sake and for its secondary solidaristic and fiscal benefits. For only when employment is plentiful and labour markets are tight is it possible for active labour market policies to fulfill their promise. Conventionally, Keynes is defunct both because fiscal resources have been exhausted, and because globalism moots

Solutions

There are two avenues of remedy: either reclaiming sovereignty for the nation-state (or the European Union) from the global market- – or inventing Keynesian institutions of reflation globally. These could be institutional or ad hoc. A common OECD commitment to reflation, a Marshall Plan-scale recovery programme for the former Soviet bloc, the creation of new cheap credits by international lending agencies, a very different operating philosophy for the GATT and IMF, would all help. Given that the current macro-economic problem is one of deflation rather than inflation, there is no excuse for failing to increase global credit and for maintaining low real interest rates. This would require a compact among the treasuries and central banks of the great powers. It would also require labour compacts to hold the rate of wage increases to that of productivy growth. Alternatively, we could very deliberately construct regional politics committed to the maintenance of a high-wage, social market economy. These would be deliberately protected by a high social tariff. Only nations within the community or with comparable social standards would enjoy completely free access to the internal market.

In some of our nations, accumulated public debt is in excess of 100% of GDP and in that sense prudent fiscal resources have probably been exhausted. It would not be sensible for, say, Italy or Canada to pursue conventional reflationary policies unilaterally. But the common credit-creating resources of the OECD nations as a whole are far from depleted. Yet most are pursuing tight-money policies that make no sense. (Lester Thurow reports conversation-sations with Bundesbank officials, in which there was general agreement that the engine of German inflation was the commitment to raise eastern German wages more rapidly than eastern German productivity, and not classical macro pressures. How, then, could tight money contribute anything more than a drag on growth? Thurow reports that the sponsors of German monetary policy could offer no theoretical justification for their current programme.) Likewise, the US Federal Reserve, in a context of almost zero inflation, falling raw materials, falling public deficits and falling real wages, insists on tightening money. A reflationary programme should be led by public investment and should be frankly aimed at restoring the virtuous circle of rising wages, rising productivity and full employment. It should aim to duplicate in peacetime the macro and micro stimulus characteristic of wars. Here is precisely where Keynes meets Schumpeter. Reflation via public investment compensates both for the loss of military Keynesianism and the loss of military Schumpeterianism. With the end of the Cold War, military-led research and development outlays and spin-off benefits of long term defense contracts are dwindling and are not being replaced by civillian outlay. Candidates for this kind of public investment include repair of basic infrastruture, as well as high-tech projects such as the 'information highway' and new high-speed rail systems. They also include investments in more environmentally benign modes of generating energy.

A new Bretton Woods would be also help. We should reform the international monetary system to discourage purely speculative movements of capital and to return to something like the Bretton Woods system. Today, more than a trillion dollars of foreign exchange trades daily, about 90% for purely speculative purposes and only about 10% to finance real commerical transactions. The system needs a tax to take the profit out of purely speculative short term money trades. It needs much stronger coordination among the major financial powers to create relatively stable currency alignments. And it needs international lending agencies willing to make available plentiful credit at low interest rates.

Trade

We need to press for a GATT system that will bring symmetry to trading relationships. Nations such as Japan that run chronic trade surpluses with the system as a whole should be subject to automatic compensatory tariffs, in the spirit of Keynes' "scarce currency" proposal to punish chronic-surplus nations because of their deflationary effect on the global system.

Free trade should be accorded nations that agree to the same basic set of rules – on market access, subsidy, intellectual property protection, anti-dumping and dispute settlement. Other nations that choose more mercantilist policies should be able to trade with the free-trade club but would be subject to moderate tariffs to compensate for the asymmetries in market openness.

Wage setting is also key. We need wage-setting models on the national or continental level that borrow from the Swedish Keynesianism of Meidner and Rehn, blending high wages with wage restraint that limits wage gains to the rate of productivity growth and rewarding labour market flexibility by taking the sting out of it for the worker, not by making it easier for employers to dispose of workers. In one sense, the wage-competition of globalisation makes the enterprise easier, since such competition changes the dynamics of the Phillips Curve. Tight national labour markets are less inflationary than they once were because of the threat of lower wage competition abroad. On the other hand, the dissolution of national oligopolies and pattern bargaining makes it more difficult to have a coherent social compact at all.

The maintenance of a high wage society is seriously undermined by laissez-faire trade. More than 60 years ago, E.F. Hecksher and Bertil Ohlin wrote that under free market conditions in trade among nations, "factor prices" will tend to converge. Generations of economics students dismissed the factor price equalization thesis because the conditions were not met. But today, as trade becomes freer and physical and financial capital more more mobile, there are indeed pressures for a downward convergence of wages.

As part of the basic rules of the trading system, social tariffs should be levied against trading partners that do not meet a basic floor of social, labour and environmental protections. Contrary to the critics of this approach, it would not harm workers in poor countries. Rather, it would put pressure on their governments and on global corporations to assure that their wages tended to rise with their productivity. This in turn would permit them to consume the equivalent of what they produced, which would be salutary for global growth. Trade could again take place – as it did during the relatively high-tariff 1950s – but would protect nations with high social standards against a 'race to the bottom'.

Recovery

None of these policies presents an easy politics. The public sector is out of fashion. Amid high unemployment, a wedge is driven between public and private sector workers; between the presumably virtuous employed and the supposedly profligate idle; between the pensioned old and the fearful young. Despite its practical failure, neo-liberalism still commands wide intellectual and ideological allegiance. The very globalism that undercuts the promise of an egalitarian, high wage society also undercuts the institutions necessary to reclaim it. But despite the new circumstances, the basic issues remain the same ones of a generation ago: how to temper market forces to allow both a full employment economy and a socially defensible distribution of income; how to use social income to manage personal transitions consistent with a broadly productive economy and sustainable family life; how to assure that technical advance provides broad benefits for ordinary people. If our governments succeed in recovering the instruments of a mixed economy, progressive politics will recover, too.

Europe: survival or decline?

5

Chris Boyd

Europe is going through a cyclical recession. The size of the European Union's economy shrank last year for the first time since the first oil crisis. But our unemployment problem is also structural. In the 1960s, Europe saw rates of unemployment of 2.5% or less: in the 1970s the average moved to around 4%; in the 1980s, the minimum reached over 8%. Although there are now hopeful signs that growth is returning to Europe, our structural problems will remain unless something is done.

We had a meagre and insufficient growth initiative in 1993. But don't underestimate its importance; it was the first time that Europe acted together. EFTA countries also played an important role. At the Copenhagen summit in the summer of 1993, Jacques Delors presented an analysis of the strengths and weaknesses of the European economy. The Heads of State and Government then requested that the Commission present a White Paper on Growth, Competitiveness and Employment. That White Paper is the subject of this chapter.

Instead of the usual esoteric subjects such as subsidiarity or budget rebates discussed at European Councils, the White Paper puts the question of employment at the top of the Union's agenda. This is what Europe should be discussing. After all, what use is the European Union if it cannot do anything about unemployment?

The White Paper presents a comprehensive framework for combatting unemployment. First, it sets an objective of creating 15m jobs by the year 2000 – which will only halve unemployment in the Union. This shows the scale of the problem before us, with some 17m unemployed in the European Union now.

Themes of the White Paper

- *Growth*. The White Paper concentrates on the structural aspects of our poor jobs performance but it does not neglect the cyclical aspects. Its analysis is that budget deficits cannot be pushed much higher, stimulus must rather come from lower interest rates.

- *Competitiveness through trans-european networks*. European's infrastructure needs to be planned on a Europe-wide basis if we are to be competitive in the 21st century. At the moment it is nationally based and under-performing compared to its main competitors.

- *Technological progress and the information society*. A revolution comparable to the invention of the printing press is taking place. Information is becoming the main raw material of tomorrow's industrial world. Our working methods are being affected (home-working, robots, lean production) and society will also be affected as communications become easier and information more accessible. We must embrace this revolution by making our economies thrive on change.

- *Education and training*. It is not through lower wages that the low-skilled will be able to compete with the newly industrialised countries of Asia and Latin America, it is through up-grading their skills. Our workers will require better education since basic literacy and numeracy will be all the more important in the information society. They will need life-long training to deal with the flexibility of new production methods and the inevitable changes required as technology progresses. The times when one skill would last a working life are gone – we will have to learn new skills and re-learn new skills several times during our working lives.

Change

We need to make our employment systems more adaptable to change. This means looking anew at the whole range of policy areas that affect the operation of the labour market, including labour law, taxation, pension rules and social security policy, to ensure that:

- equity objectives are achived in a way that does not adversely affect the functioning of labour market;

- labour market regulation, housing or other policies do not act as a constraint on labour mobility;

- obstacles to more flexible working time are dismantled.

Reducing non-wage costs for the low-skilled

The low paid are particularly hard hit by unemployment. They are competing now in our increasingly global economy with workers elsewhere on much lower wages. Yet we still tax labour as a factor of production very highly – a left-over from the 1960s when labour was scarce. In many countries of the Union non-wage costs are actually regressive – in other words, the non-wage costs for low paid workers are a greater proportion of total costs than for the higher paid.

This is not sensible. The White Paper therefore suggests that non-wage costs be cut, especially for the low-paid. In compensation for this, since budget deficits should not rise, there should be higher taxes on pollution. In this way some of the tax burden could be shifted from the abundant resource, labour, towards the scarce resource, a clean environment.

Active labour market policies

Research done by the Commission and the experience of many countries, particularly in Scandinavia, shows the advantage of concentrating resources on active labour market policies. Rather than paying the unemployed to do nothing, they should be encouraged intensively to search for a new job, retrain, or even do something socially useful. There are many countries in the Union that need to spend more on active labour market policies, now that jobs are beginning to be created once more, to help prevent bottlenecks emerging and thus to help non-inflationary growth. The Commission has proposed a Youth Start scheme, designed to help prevent the young from becoming long-term unemployed, by offering them a training place or activity.

Implementation

An Action Plan was agreed at the Brussels summit in December 1993. It is up to us to ensure that it is carried through.

- The internal market needs completion, particularly in the areas of telecoms and energy. And its rules must be enforced – especially on state aids and competition.

- A group of personal representatives of the Heads of Government is working on the definition of a set of priority projects in the transeuropean networks. It has agreed a set of 11 priority projects that will start within two years.

- A new 12.3bn ecu research and development programme has been agreed to ensure that Community research efforts are maintained at a high level.

Information society

The European Council set up a group of experts under the chairmanship of Martin Bangemann to look into the issue of the 'information society'. Are we in the midst of a revolution? If so, what should we do about it? We will be overtaken by our competitors unless we liberalise our telecoms industries and allow new initiatives and ideas to flourish. Also, the regulatory side is important: we must put in place a simple, clear and stable regulatory framework that ensures interoperability and protects rights. Do we need to spend large amounts on the infrastructure? The groups think not. It is the services (electonic images, access to databases, electronic mail) and applications (teleworking, teletraining, tele-medecine) that really need to be developed. These may require a certain pump-priming by, for example, links between administrations.

Change of decor

This could have been the subtitle of the White Paper. What does it mean? We are changing, but the world around us is changing faster than we are in various aspects: technological progress; globalisation; the information society; the environment; time (researchers tell us that our working lives will fall from 70,000 to 40,000 hours – we shall need to get away from the old concept of an age for learning, an age for working and an age for rest).

The White Paper is an attempt to look at these long-term questions and suggest ways to manage the changes ahead of us. One goal was to combat short-termism. Environment, social policy (drugs, crime, poverty), financial markets, education, politics are all examples of areas in which the short-term view tends to dominate.

The White Paper is not a blueprint but a first attempt to think about the longer term changes that we must undergo if we are not to face economic and social decline. It involves various themes, each with the idea that we cannot go on as we are:

- underuse of labour, overuse of environmental resources;

- social versus individual costs (internal versus external flexibility such as firms treating unemployment as though it were costless when it does impose a cost – on society);

We should learn from 'green' accounting. The current transportation system, for example, costs 3-4% of GDP in pollution, traffic jams and accidents, yet this is not taken into account when measuring GDP.

Clean, environmentally friendly technology is a key. One of the externalites that is often forgotten when the economics is discussed is 'first mover advantage' – the competitive jump-start that our industries will have in this growth field if we impose the environmental standards first.

The White paper looks at various paths of change:

- internalising external costs and benefits (market incentives);
- research into environmentally clean technologies;
- ensuring that environmental aspects become part of the trade agenda;
- sectoral policies will be affected (energy, transport, agriculture,industry);
- the implementation of CO_2/energy tax is all the more vital;
- employment creation could be substantial in environment sector.

Employment is at the top of the European Union's agenda, where it belongs; hopefully short-termism has been halted and we have lifted our sights.

The White Paper is not a blueprint, it is a suggested framework that, we hope, will encourage the debate and promote the actions necessary if we are to overcome the waste and the misery of unemployment.

Economic security and minimum labour standards

6

John Evans

In 1947, the UN Conference on Trade and Employment held in Havana sought to do to the international trading system what the Bretton Woods Conference three years earlier had done to the financial system – to establish an institutional framework to encourage the growth of trade and avoid the return of the 'beggar my neighbour' trade wars of the 1930's. By an historical accident, however, the international institution whose creation was agreed – the International Trade Organisation (ITO) – never saw the light of day. In 1948 the US Senate failed to ratify the Charter and the ITO was never created.

The ITO's demise was of more than just academic interest because its founding Charter included a 'Social Clause' committing ITO members to observe fair labour standards. To this day the Havana Charter remains the clearest multilateral governmental statement of the linkage between trade and labour standards.

Article 7 reads: "The members recognise that measures relating to employment must take fully into account the rights of workers under inter-governmental declarations, conventions and agreements. They recognise that all countries have a common interest in the achievement and maintenance of fair labour standards related to productivity, and thus in the improvement of wages and working conditions as productivity may permit. The members recognise that unfair labour conditions, particularly in product for export, create difficulties in international trade, and accordingly, each member shall take whatever action may be appropriate and feasible to eliminate such conditions within its territory".

With the demise of the ITO, the gap was filled by the far more limited General Agreement on Tariffs and Trade (GATT) but the multilateral linkage between trade and labour standards was lost for the immediate post war period.

All embracing

The clarity of the debate has not been helped by far too many issues being grouped under the heading of 'international labour standards'. There are, for instance, different issues involved in discussing the social dimension of European Union integration and in discussing a Social Clause in multilateral trade agreements. Different approaches will, obviously, be necessary. In countries of comparable economic development and strength – especially those engaged in full scale economic integration such as the European Union – harmonisation of labour standards and labour legislation is bound to take place. The real issue is whether this emphasises the best, rather than the worst, practice. As the July 1994 *OECD Employment Outlook* pointed out, high labour standards in industrialised countries tend to be associated with high levels of productivity and are far from inconsistent with economic efficiency and competitiveness. Without an effective social dimension European economic union may, in the short term, put downward pressure on standards.

At a global level wide differences exist in productivity, living standards and institutional structures. And since the international trade union movement does not advocate a global minimum wage, a Social Clause is intended to establish a global commitment to the observation of basic worker rights (rather than the specification of the standards resulting from the free exercise of those rights). It is not for developed countries to dictate to the developing world what their levels of wages should be – but it is legitimate that they should insist that the populations of all trading countries have the right to form trade unions which can then negotiate those conditions. We should put our faith in trade unions. As the experience of South Africa has shown, once trade union freedoms are granted and established, a thriving and effective set of social institutions is not far behind.

Growth

A Social Clause would not keep imports from developing countries out of OECD markets because they are produced with lower labour costs – it is not about slowing the development process. However, economic growth and increased trade will not automatically 'trickle down' to the populations of developing countries and lead to more jobs and social progress. Where basic rights are denied and power is concentrated in the hands of a political and economic elite, this itself will restrict the ability of mass markets to appear in developing countries. For growing trade to lead to benefits for the population of developing countries as a whole there must be freedom to create institutions such as trade unions that can ensure a fair distribution of productivity gains. This is also, of course, in the interest of the whole world trade system by encouraging the faster growth of new markets.

Fundamental

The need for basic trade union rights and a Social Clause was brought home graphically to me at a much more fundamental level when I attended a meeting in Thailand in June 1993 shortly after the Kader toy factory fire which cost the lives of 188 (mainly women) workers and injured almost 500 others. Kader is a Hong Kong owned multinational which subcontracts toy production to many sites in Asia for sale to western markets through well known retail outlets. When their factory near Bangkok caught fire on 10 May 1993, few of the workers escaped as there were no fire exits, sprinklers or alarms. Other exits were locked and the windows barred. As in many Asian factories, the building looked more like a prison than a workplace. The unions representing the families who lost relatives in the fire were, understandably, initially concerned with the difficulty of getting compensation from the multinational. Yet when posed with the real issue of how to avoid disasters being repeated, the unions appeared fatalistic at the scale of the task. A Social Clause would go some way to putting pressure on the government and the employers to recognise free trade unions and observe basic health and safety standards. The right to elect safety and union representatives, independent of management, to ensure that factory doors are unlocked and fire safety procedures exist would do little to undermine the competitiveness of Thai toy factories – but it would save lives.

Restrictions

Organising trade unions in many parts of the world remains a hazardous process. The establishment of 'free trade' or 'export processing zones' is undermining even further the limited labour rights which exist. Pakistan's 1992 Finance Act allows labour legislation in certain regions to be suspended by government announcement. Columbia, Peru and Venezuela all have restricted labour legislation in export zones. National unions are forbidden from organising in Malaysia's export electronics industry.

The developing world is also blighted by child labour. Two hundred million children are estimated to work as cheap labour under appalling conditions. They are robbed of their childhood and often their health and yet governments are increasingly turning a blind eye. Whilst child labour is often posed as an alternative to even greater poverty for an individual family, it is simply not an acceptable alternative. It is also robbing the countries themselves of the resource they most desperately need – an educated adult labour force.

Democracy or autocracy?

The real difference of view over a Social Clause is therefore between those who believe that the creation of democratic institutions is a necessary aid to development and those who believe that autocratic government and 'disciplined' labour is the key to economic success. Prime Minister Mahathir of Malaysia has the great asset of not fudging his views and put the anti-democratic case clearly in an interview with *The Wall Street Journal* in 1993. In support of his view that suppressing unions is necessary for trade, he said: "We worry about our workers. Once you insist workers have the right to strike, they don't know how far to go". But the tragic lesson of the last 50 years is rather that once governments get authoritarian powers they don't know how far to go.

On the other side of the argument are more than just the international trade union movement and human rights groups. In December 1993, the OECD's Development Assistance Committee published *Guidelines for Aid Donors on Participatory Development and Good Governance*, drawing the firm conclusion that development efforts can no longer rely on 'top-down' government but have to focus on building up independent and democratic institutions. The guidelines urged governments to support the activities of independent bodies (including trade unions) and stressed the importance of observing the ILO Conventions on trade union rights.

Some more far sighted employers have also begun to raise the issue of the responsibility of multinational companies in relation to human rights. The Sullivan Code, concerning the operations of American companies in South Africa in the 1980's, had a positive impact. More recently, the clothing manufacturer Levi's has scaled back its operations in China because of the prevalence of forced labour. But unless international rules are established the danger remains that trade liberalisation will accelerate the 'rush to the bottom' in the short term.

Rules

The rules that have to be drawn up by the WTO have been clearly identified by the international trade union movement. They cover the six basic rights in the Conventions of the International Labour Organisation:

- freedom of association (ILO Convention 87);

- the right of collective bargaining (Convention 98);

- the prohibition of forced labour (ILO Conventions 29 and 105);

- a minimum age for employment (ILO Convention 138);

- non-discrimination in employment (ILO Conventions 100 and 111).

There is also a case for examining the procedural aspects of health and safety standards (such as ILO Convention 150). These Conventions are equally relevant for all countries. Their observance would do much to allow trade expansion to bring about an improvement of basic conditions of life. They would also stop the violation of some of the most fundamental human rights.

Members of the WTO should commit themselves to the observance of these basic Conventions as if the Havana Charter been adopted. But there must be an implementation mechanism established. One possibility would be the creation of a joint committee between the WTO and ILO. On receipt of a complaint from any of the constituents of the ILO, an examination would be undertaken to see whether the country was meeting its obligations regarding the Social Clause. Should it be found to be falling short of its obligations, the Committee would recommend measures to be taken within a specific time period, for example two years. Within that period the ILO would offer technical assistance to help the country meet its obligations. Following the specified period a report would be made on the extent to which progress was being made or setting out a timetable for action. As a last resort sanctions could be applied if a country consistently refused to comply.

It is hard to see how such a multilateral process could be manipulated for protectionist ends; indeed, it looks a far more desirable route to follow than the escalation of unilateral and bilateral measures of trade sanctions against individual countries in the light of public outcry against human rights abuses. Such an implementation mechanism also looks mild compared to the original sanctions proposed for the ILO by the Lloyd George government in 1919 at the time of the establishment of the ILO. The original British first draft of the ILO Constitution said: "One of the major aims of the international Conventions is the eradication of unfair competition, which is founded on oppressive working conditions. The appropriate penalty should be that if a two thirds majority of the conference has reached the conclusion that the stipulations of the Convention have been disregarded, the signatory states should discriminate against the goods produced under proven conditions of unfair competition unless those conditions are eradicated within one year or a longer period to be determined by Conference".

The Social Clause can only be one element of a wider approach to building social rules into a more globalised world economy. Implementation of the OECD's Development Assistance Committee guidelines could ensure that resources and financial incentives are available to assist countries to meet their obligations. Efforts are underway in the US Congress to make funding from the IMF and World Bank conditional on respect for basic rights. For the last decade, unions have sought more effective implementation of codes of conduct on investment such as the OECD *Guidelines on Multinational Enterprises*. As OECD membership is expanding, the Trades Union Advisory Committee is seeking to ensure that new members observe the organisation's basic standards of human rights. All of this is designed to ensure that the new economic and social 'model' which is appearing (particularly in parts of Asia), combining market economics and political suppression, is countered. The lesson of Eastern Europe was that central planning and political dictatorship did not produce a workers' paradise; but the combination of free markets and political dictatorship will certainly produce a workers' hell.

Working women: time for new approaches

7

Linda Tarr-Whelan

Women in the economy are an essential ingredient in questions of future economic growth as they near the point of being half the workforce. Any country that ignores the phenomena of working women – or subsumes it under the rubric of 'all workers' – does so at its peril. The national competitive edge in a global 'information age' economy is the knowledge, skills and abilities of workers.

Women workers are important to the design of national jobs and economic growth strategies. Governments are often hampered in exploring policy options by their myopic view of the status quo as a male preserve. Instead, they can solve economic and political difficulties creatively by revising economic policy as if women mattered.

There is much to be done. As long as close to half the workforce faces discrimination, is consistently undervalued and segregated into certain jobs or forced to choose unnecessarily between work and family then we all lose as the income of families and the health of the economy decline.

The world of work has changed. The realities of family life have changed. There is common ground among women – and in many cases between women and men – that bread-and-butter issues are at the top of the list. It is time for new approaches.

Who produces economic growth?

Although largely invisible, the power of the American economy is increasingly underpinned by women workers and women entrepreneurs:

- Women are 45.6% of the workforce now and projected to be 47% by 2005. Women experienced their highest labour force participation rate at 57.8% in 1992 and accounted for 60% of the total labour force growth between 1982 and 1992. That trend is expected to continue until 2005 (*US Department of Labor Women's Bureau*).

- By the end of this year it is projected that there will be more Americans employed by women-owned businesses than by the Fortune 500 companies (*Foundation of Women Business Owners, 1992*).

- In 1991, nearly two-thirds of women in the labour force were single (25%), divorced (12%), widowed or separated (8%) or had husbands with 1990 income of less than $17,500 (17.7%) (*US Department of Labor Women's Bureau, 1991*).

- Women's work is a significant part of family income. In 1991, the median income of married-couple families with the wife in the paid labour force was $48,169 compared to $30,075 for families without the wife in the paid labour force and $16,692 for families headed by single women (*US Department of Commerce, Bureau of Labor Statistics, 1991*).

Family incomes have stagnated despite mothers being in the workforce. Of all families with children, the percentage with two parents (or the only parent) in the labour force rose from 56% in 1980 to 66% in 1991 (*Select Committee on Children, Youth and Families, US House of Representatives, 1992*). In that year, 58% of married women worked outside the home in comparison to 25% in 1950 (*US Department of Labor, 'Employment and Earnings', 1992*). More than 8 out of 10 women with children over 11 years of age are in the workforce (*CPA, 'Women's Voices', 1992*).

Women overwhelmingly work in traditional 'women's jobs'. In 1988, only 9% of all working women were employed in jobs which are non-traditional, defined as occupational categories where 75% or more of those employed are men (*National Commission on Working Women, 1990*). Despite considerable angst that the increase of women in the labour market has decreased wages or jobs for men, the worlds of work for men and women are still quite separate.

Wage gap

There is a wage gap in virtually every occupation and at virtually every level, regardless of education, experience or seniority. Female-male wage ratios are virtually the same for those workers with no interruptions in employment as for all workers (*National Committee on Pay Equity, 1989*).

On March 13, 1994, the *Washington Post* published an article on the importance of education to workers' income over their lifetime. But it revealed two other stories: first, how little education counts in raising wages for women;

and second, that the closing of the wage gap between women and men has been largely the result of the decline of men's wages, not increases for women.

The foregone revenue for women embedded in the wage gap is extraordinary. The women's movement in America has popularized concern about the wage gap by talking about the 'pennies per hour' difference between women and men – women now earn 71 cents for every dollar earned by a man. However, this approach hides the enormous gap in annual salaries and makes the yawning canyon between the worklives of women and men seem fairly insignificant. Instead, closing that gap could have enormous consequences for women.

There is an average of more than $400,000 difference in income over the worklife of college educated men and women – a number which dwarfs the supplementary income and social welfare supports traditionally discussed as essential for 'helping' women. Over a lifetime of 40 years of work, American college graduate women can expect an average of $420,000 less than male college graduates. That is the result of $13,000 a year average earnings gap: $26,000 for women and $39,000 for men (*Women's Voices, 1992*).

Lamentably, ours is a society where the level of one's salary is considered a strong indicator of worth. In the US, machines and money are the realm of men's work while people and services are women's work. And we can clearly see what is valued. Over the long term, the undervaluing of the enterprise of caregiving is particularly destructive to women workers and community well-being.

Women's wages are suppressed and few efforts have been made to change these dynamics. Comparable worth initiatives have made inroads only in some public jurisdictions. Unionized women earn $2.50 more per hour than non-unionized women (*Institute for Women's Policy Research*) although union membership is still sliding.

In many cases, market dynamics in scarce women's occupations have been met with substitution of cheaper labour (nursing), automation (secretarial work) and part-time, contingent arrangements rather than full-time work with better salaries and benefits.

Part-time work, a convenient management option to increase flexibility and decrease labour costs, is also largely a women's reality. Women comprise two-thirds of the part-time workforce (*Bureau of Labor Statistics, 1991*). The rate of involuntary part-timers (workers who would prefer full-time hours) is 44% higher for women than men (*Economic Policy Institute, 1990*). The average part-time worker earns only 60% of the hourly wage of the average full-time worker and benefits also lag.

Women workers have poured into the labour market at a time when productivity gains – which have been substantial in the US in recent times – have gone largely to shareholders in dividend checks rather being than invested in the workforce (or research, plant or equipment). Now the federal government expects to 'downsize' by 250,000 workers over the next few years following the private sector trend toward massive layoffs.

Female entrepreneurs

Perhaps the most dramatic figures of economic energy are the figures about women entrepreneurs. Women business owners are the fastest growing sector of the business community – now making up 32% of small business ownership, up from 5% in 1970 (*Small Business Administration, 1992*). Small businesses are variously defined in the US and these figures are based on businesses with less than 500 employees. Others use 50 or 100 employees as the definition of 'small' and describe businesses between that size and 500 as 'medium'.

The importance of businesses with less than 500 employees to the American economy is considerable. In some states, Vermont and Wyoming for example, nearly 100% of all private sector workers are employed in smaller firms (*CPA, 1993*). In 1991, only 39% of American workers were employed in firms larger than 50 workers (*Women's Legal Defense Fund, 1992*).

This sector is increasingly important to workers. Between 1977-87, the proportion of private sector employment in firms of over 500 employees declined from 43.3% to 28.7% of total employment (*Department of Commerce, 1992*). This trend has clearly accelerated with large-scale industrial 'downsizing' and defence cut-backs. Progressive strategies for growth cannot depend upon the stabilization of larger (although more likely unionized) businesses.

The growth of women-owned small businesses is particularly important. Many women have entered this area to "create my own job", when 'women's work' pays less than poverty wages or where few jobs exist; to balance family and work; or to escape the unfriendly atmosphere for women in corporate life. The annual receipts of women-owned business are greater than those of any single state in the nation and quadrupled between 1982 and 1987 (*National Foundation for Women Business Owners, 1992*).

There are a variety of projections about the growth of women-owned small businesses, with the advocates expecting the proportion to be 50% by 2000 (*National Association of Women's Business Advocates, 1994*) and the Small Business Administration expecting it to be 40% by 2000 (*SBA, 1994*). From 1982 to 1987 the rate of growth in total receipts for women-owned businesses was four times that of all businesses (*National Women's Business Council testimony, 1994*).

In an interesting harbinger of the future, women choose self-employment at a rate five times greater than men and are successful in 80% of the business they begin. A recent Gallup Poll showed that almost half of women aged 35-54 want to start a business; with women between 18-34 the number rises to almost two-thirds (*US Department of Labor Glass Ceiling Commission, 1994*)

What do women want?

In late 1992 the Center for Policy Alternatives and the Ms. Foundation jointly commissioned the first national American survey of women's economic lives since 1985 and the first such work done by a team of women. This bi-partisan poll was widely reported and was the subject of briefings for both Bill Clinton and George Bush.

Since that time, CPA has co-sponsored two national women's economic summits in 1992 and 1994. The reports of both have been presented to the Clinton Economic Summit (during the transition) or the White House. The voices of American women tell us they want and expect:

- Economic policy to be framed as if women counted, with full recognition of the new realities of men and women at work.

- Family economic security, not just sectoral analysis.

- Practical 'Main Street' and 'kitchen table' concerns having parity with 'Wall Street' solutions and international finance.

- Economic equality, with meaningful choices for merging family and work.

- Policies based on the strength and importance of women to the economy, not a dependency social welfare model.

At the 1994 Women's Economic Summit we focused on the top three important facets of women's economic lives as identified by our previous work: entrepreneurial expansion, sustained economic survival, and family and work balance. We sought to build a common vision for a different economic future for women and their families, not simply a set of technical solutions.

Agenda

The energetic consensus-building process among women leaders from the grassroots, politics, government, corporate and small business sectors had strong themes:

- Women are together on the economic and social agenda for the US, with family economic security and well-being as the top issues.

- Our issues are no longer just 'women's issues'. We bring a new set of values to build a vibrant American economy in the global marketplace.

- Investment in people, families and communities will build a stronger social fabric for long-term economic growth.

- Government and the private sector must do more with incentives and long term investments that recognize human as well as financial returns. With essentially no new Federal dollars, we must spend our public resources effectively to meet our values.

- A new definition of infrastructure is evolving. In order for all of us to work productively, we need community-based, family care services, not just roads, bridges and communication systems.

- The choice between economic growth and a workplace that invests in families and communities is a false choice. A healthy economy and healthy families are inextricably linked. To strengthen the overall bottom line, we can – and must – have both.

- The values of tomorrow, with more women in leadership positions, strengthen America. Capital and information are no longer bound by national borders; our competitive edge is the quality, skill, diversity, and knowledge of our people.

Nowhere was the consensus clearer than in the session on our common values. A vision of society emerged in which a focus on all stakeholders – shareholders, employees, families and communities – replaces a sole focus on the shareholder; in which empowering, flexible, responsive structures replace 'command and control' hierarchical structures; in which an investment and long term profit perspective replaces a focus on cost and short term profit; in which open and easy access to the resources to build success replaces closed, 'old boy' structures; in which prevention replaces crisis response; in which sustainable self-sufficiency replaces charity...in which conserving, developing and building resources replaces consuming and disposing of resources; and in which the commitment to equity makes inequity unacceptable.

The polling data in *Women's Voices* told us that for all women "making ends meet" and "balancing family and work" are their greatest concerns, regardless of geographic differences, ethnicity, age or political party. All other 'women's issues' had much less saliency than family economic security with a strong consensus around universal health care, equal pay and the balance between family and work. Women, much more than men, saw a major role for government in improving people's lives.

Our work has led the Center for Policy Alternatives to create a policy agenda for the 'New Economy' which affirms women's values. It includes a new definition of infrastructure to include the services which are necessary in communities where most parents are in the workforce; making work pay (including care-giving) not as a social program but an economic one; family-friendly policies and a harassment-free workplace; and access to capital and networks for women entrepreneurs.

Empowering women to take their place in economic decision-making can change our society. The values which bring women together are the basis of a new approach to building communities and an economy which clearly values the work of women and strengthens family security.

Community capital: jobs from the bottom-up

8

Richard C. Ferlauto

Emphasising job growth through major public expenditures misses an important opportunity. Progressives now have the chance to craft an alternative vision that builds a political consensus and communities, through economic development.

In any event, large public outlays are not on the political agenda. But even if they were, we would ignore community economic development strategies at our peril. Beyond the question of present political acceptability lies the fact that public spending policies as a means for job creation may be hitting their limit in the new economy of the 21st century. Certainly, they leave some constituencies or geographic regions completely behind. National public spending and borrowing programmes are no longer sufficient remedies for stagnant wages to reach full employment.

New technologies are transforming all areas of work in manufacturing, service and information delivery. The globalization of production, mobility of capital and almost instantaneous access to information create two seemingly divergent changes in the structure of economic activity. First, production is increasingly organized on a global scale beyond the influence of national spending programs. In 1990, the largest 100 firms in the world had over $3.1 trillion in assets, of which nearly 40% were invested outside of the firm's home country. Almost $1 trillion in currency transactions occur every day. National borders no longer define complete financial systems and hence national employment stimulus from the multiplier effect of public spending becomes diluted.

Second, the primary drivers of economic development in the US are decisions made at a more local level with the 50 states being key. Micro level policy aimed at job creation involves decisions about education, infrastructure, tax policy, public subsidies and availability of capital – all determined in the US more locally than nationally. At this level the debate between 'trickle down' and re-distribution policies is less important than understanding the basic questions that communities consider when planning for economic development. What are the strategies for attracting capital? What are the values communities use to reach a consensus on those strategies? The question of values is the key. Political choices based on commonly held values make the difference between a low wage economy and expanding economic opportunities for all.

For progressives it is by working with community capital and using the tools of community economic development that will forge a national constituency around families and community economic security. Our role is to define and show by example how communities connect to the global financial system in ways that private capital does not. As we know too well, in America private capital can force communities to compete against one another based on low wages and low taxes. We need to focus on re-positioning financial markets to offer incentives to investments targeted to local economic development and to penalize short term speculation. Creation of an expanded base of community capital – our alternative vision – can add value to production and create opportunities for higher wage jobs and a higher standard of living for all communities, not just a few winners.

Lack of support for public investment strategies

Following Bill Clinton's Economic Summit in December 1991 progressives enthusiastically supported his call for a national stimulus package. After the Congressional dust settled the result was an anemic program, well short of the boost necessary to create any significant growth in employment. A victory would have been an important symbol for labour and liberals. In the media, and before Congress, the Clinton package represented 'pork-barrel' interest group politics, rather than a 'good jobs alternative' to the plans of Republicans. In the end, in the battle between budget deficits and public sector stimulus, the new president was forced to back down.

In a quick change of direction, the stimulus program was traded for a hard line on deficit spending and a pact with Federal Reserve Chairman Alan Greenspan to bring interest rates down to their lowest point in twenty years (before they started rising again). The US economy has responded by producing substantial numbers of new but low paying jobs. For every American who prospered during the 1980's, two lost ground. Worker income declined by 17%, while rental housing costs increased by 238%. Many American families have had to trade higher paying 'men's' manufacturing jobs for two less well paying jobs to maintain their family standard of living. In the 1992 Presidential campaign, Tom Harkin used the example of the factory worker who made $18/hour with excellent benefits before he was laid off. He now makes $7.50/hour and his wife makes $4.50/hour, collectively working double the number of hours per week for three-quarters of the income.

Within the context of new job development, sectoral unemployment remains a substantial problem. Black unemployment is triple that of whites and urban youth unemployment averages over 50%. Employment opportunities for women are stuck on the low end of the wage scale.

The community-based economic development alternative

The concept of community capital – targeted private investment that adds value to communities beyond a short term return to stock holders – is central to a bottom up approach to job creation. Here, the role of government is not that of public stimulus but catalyst. By implementing policies that regulate capital flight, reward job-creating investments and build capacity at the community level to connect private dollars to economic development opportunities, government leverages scarce public dollars.

The underlying principle is to give families and communities the tools and resources needed successfully to compete and cooperate in an expanded economic future. This approach to job growth emanates from the values of democratic citizen participation and economic organisation at the local and regional level.

The Right understands the saliency and power of micro economics with the public. Their simple analysis works well as a conservative manifesto: cut business taxes, offer corporate incentives, dismantle government mandates and provide voucher systems that weaken broad public institutions such as education. In the US, the Jack Kemp-led Republican 'empowerment' agenda set the initial terms of the debate because it rings true with many of our traditional constituencies: "return control to local communities to determine their own futures". So far, liberals have done a poor job in responding by overly relying on federal spending solutions which the public distrusts.

As progressives we have to be able to offer an alternative vision for how local economies can succeed. Linda Tarr-Whelan writes in Chapter 7 about *family* security. Micro economic strategies are about *community* security. The policy elements of this bottom-up approach are described below and include:

- creating community capital through regulating private capital flows with community reinvestment acts; capitalizing community development financial institutions; and economically targeted investing of institutional investments;

- developing community-based economic development alternatives and building a nonprofit sector for housing and community development which offers an alternative to the private sector without the bureaucracy of a centralized government delivery mechanism.

Creating community capital

The cry for increased capital resounds across the US today. The fires of Los Angeles in 1993 only highlighted the problem of disinvestment that has plagued our urban areas for decades. Throughout the US the lack of access to capital constrains growth. According to studies by the Federal Reserve, minorities are twice as likely as whites to be denied mortgage loans even when the lack of income is removed as a factor. Studies of the flow of bank deposits indicate that both urban and rural areas have a net outflow of deposits made in banks.

Access to capital is the key to economic activity in urban neighborhoods. The total capital demand for minority-owned businesses exceeds $140 billion annually. We see that the number of black owned businesses have declined by 50% per capita since 1970. Without incentives or regulations, the financial system will not meet the community need for credit while the demand for global capital is enormous.

Banks are not investing their assets directly in communities. The Federal Reserve reports that bank holdings of government securities have risen from $459.5 billion in 1991 to $656.5 billion in 1993, while business loans decreased from $638.1 billion to $538 billion.

A consolidated financial services industry has emerged in which money management decisions occur far away from communities. Investment decisions hold no regard for long term community health and are made based on quarterly profits. The Saving and Loans scandal in the US of the mid 1980's was only the most egregious example of deregulated financial institutions going on holiday at government expense using government insured deposits in highly speculative non-productive endeavors. The Wall Street short-term profit investment culture promotes community disinvestment and de-industrialization.

A community capital agenda gives priority to long-term community asset building over short-term profit taking. It can mean big money – much more than current public budgets for economic investing. In the US, a broad network of community based organizations, urban and minority political leaders, housing activists and small business associations are the core constituents of a public program for public capital. The Clinton Administration has taken some interesting small steps in the right direction. With support, the political movement for these reforms could be magnified many times.

Community Reinvestment Acts

In the US, Federal and state Community Reinvestment Acts require that banks serve the credit needs of the communities in which they operate as a condition for business as a chartered institution. The Federal CRA, established in 1977, was conceived as a way to keep money in urban neighbourhoods by ending discrimination in mortgage lending practices. The law was virtually ignored by federal bank regulators during twelve years of Republican administrations. During that time, a widespread, locally-based grassroots movement used the law to negotiate community lending agreements with banks who sought to merge or otherwise expand their activities.

Based on the success of these community lending agreements, some banks began to change their orientation and now see community lending as a growing market niche. Between 1988 and 1992 banks had made $35 billion dollars in lending commitments to low income neighborhoods. Most recently, national financial services companies including NationsBank, Fleet and Bank of America have agreed to community lending programs over the next few years in which they have each committed $10 billion.

Perhaps Bill Clinton's most unheralded accomplishment is his effort to put more teeth into community reinvesting. In July 1993 he called on Federal bank regulators to rewrite CRA rules and design a bank evaluation system for community lending based on specific lending goals. CRA laws are being expanded at the federal and state levels to specific target lending to small businesses, community development organizations and community facilities such as child care.

Similarly, Congress has also moved to make Government Sponsored Entities – 'Fannie Mae' and 'Freddie Mac' (the large private corporations that create secondary markets with implied government guarantees) – more accountable for making mortgage capital available for low income urban areas. Although they are charged with creating liquidity in the mortgage markets, community lending has now becomes a core part of their business. In March 1994, Fannie Mae announced a $1 trillion expansion into the affordable mortgage market. Access to mortgage credit has a large stimulative effect on employment: every $1 billion in single family housing investments supports approximately 25,000 jobs (*University of Maryland*).

Community development financial institutions

Wall Street capital and major institutional investors function as wholesale institutions with very limited ability to deliver retail capital to 'Main Street', where it is most needed. Community development financial institutions can connect wholesale (global) capital to localities. In the US, a network of credit unions, 'micro loan' funds, community development loan funds and community development banks are emerging that combine retailing capital with financial management, business training and risk management. They have the potential to replace traditional community lenders in their support of business development.

During his campaign, President Clinton spoke about creating a national network of 200 community development banks based on the successes of the South Shore Bank in Chicago and the Elkhorn Bank in rural Arkansas. The South Shore Bank and its holding company have revitalized a declining neighborhood by providing access to credit and technical assistance to small businesses and housing developers. But Clinton's original proposal has now shrunk to a very small legislative initiative with a $500 million appropriation.

The community development bank model is supplemented by a newly energized group of 350 micro loan funds that provide capital to very small entrepreneurs. This dynamic network includes women, immigrants and minorities who see small businesses as a way out of poverty. While initial jobs are low-paying they are also the first step up the ladder of opportunity. With training, credit and access, business networkers and micro-businesses stimulate economy activity in depressed areas that are otherwise cut off from the economic mainstream.

The Center for Self Help in North Carolina (which began as a Micro lender) has developed a portfolio of over 600 community development loans valued at more than $20 million dollars. In over 15 years they never had a default. Based on this record of success, the Center has recently closed a deal to purchase $20 million of affordable housing loans from a regional bank.

Economically targeted investment

Pension funds, mutual funds and insurance companies – the largest holders of capital assets in the US today – are potential sources of financing for housing, infrastructure and economic development that are available to fill the credit gaps created by changes in the financial services industry. Pension funds alone have assets totalling over $4.4 trillion. Of that total, public pension systems have nearly $1 trillion in assets while union plans hold another $500 billion. Pension funds own almost 39% of all outstanding equity in American firms and 50% of all corporate bonds. The 4,000 mutual funds in the US grow at a rate of $25 billion a month. With approximately $1.8 trillion in assets, the US Department of the Treasury closely scrutinizes their rapid expansion as money pours in from insured bank deposits.

5% from these two investors would provide over $300 billion that could be targeted to community economic development. Economically Targeted Investments (ETIs) earn risk adjusted market rates of return, while providing a collateral benefit to a geographic region or industry by creating housing, jobs or filling an identifiable capital gap. Public pension systems in the US increasingly view ETIs as investment options. Over the past five years, 27 state public retirement systems have invested about $20 billion into ETIs. Four states have created specific pension fund intermediaries for economic development.

Economic targeting has become a major issue for pension systems in America. The Clinton Administration has embraced the concept and the Secretary of the Department of Housing and Urban Development (HUD) has organized an ETI Task Force to create new investment opportunities. A new joint venture between the AFL-CIO and HUD will use $600 million in union pension funds to build 10,000 housing units while creating 12,000 jobs for union members.

The National Infrastructure Investment Commission has identified pension funds as the primary source of funds to capitalize a national development bank. Federal government infrastructure investment had declined from 2.3% of GNP in 1963 to 1% in 1989. An infrastructure development program that leverages pension funds backed by local guarantees and/or income streams could be viable at a state or regional level. Such a micro-stimulus strategy should combine mass transportation and road improvement (including set-asides for women and minority owned contractors) with human services facility development (child care and community health centers).

Community-based economic development

In the US, economic development programmes have traditionally been state-based efforts at industrial recruitment. Throughout the 1950's and '60s, 'smokestack chasing' states in the South raided the Northern states by offering tax concessions, low-income and business taxes and non-union work places. Now the Southern states are hit as large corporations can move to South America or Asia seeking ever lower wages. States are beginning to seek place-determined alternatives by enhancing their own capital and human resources for job creation. They are reprogramming expenditures for industrial recruitment into efforts that create wealth that will not pick-up and move.

Between 1980 and 1986, half the jobs created in the US were in firms of 100 or fewer employees. Small business and self-employment have been critical, not only for upward mobility but for growth of the economy as a whole. Two-thirds of all new jobs are created by small business and over 90% of America's businesses are small.

The Clinton Administrations recently unveiled an 'Empowerment Zone and Enterprise Communities initiative which embodies these principles of bottom-up development, coordinated through a public planning process to leverage private sector involvement. The competitive grant effort is very small and targets only the nation's most devastated communities which really need substantially more resources than are contained in the initiative. But the President's attention to healthy communities must be acknowledged. Healthy communities promote and improve the personal relationships that can build consensus around investing in itself and should be a focus for our activism.

Building alternatives

The viable alternative to large scale public projects is to rebuild connections between private capital and community needs, using public policy as the catalyst and community-based developers as the brokers of economic change. In the austere 1980s, over 2,000 community-based development organizations (frequently non-profits) sprouted and grew in poor communities. In turn, they have seeded and supported over 2,000 new enterprises, created or saved over 100,000 jobs, built over 320,000 units of housing and developed 17 million square feet of office space. The more experienced groups have learned how to combine enterprise development, housing development, child care and social services.

The community-based developers have demonstrated the power of giving people a stake in the outcome of developments. They draw on public capital but then use it to leverage private investment. They are efficient intermediaries because they are nonprofit as well as entrepreneurial. They are a new private sector that pursues public goals.

For progressives, the alternative of developing community capital to deliver jobs from the bottom-up is an effective way to build both democratic participation and community strength. In a time where there is little public support for the traditional public stimulus packages, using public money as a catalyst to leverage large scale private investment at the local level is essential to economic growth.

Full employment in a free society

9

Will Hutton and Robert Kuttner

After a quarter-century of steady growth and near-full employment, the years since 1973 have brought slower growth, steadily rising unemployment, widening inequality and escalating social distress. Fiscally, these conditions have produced an overload on the state, which has been called upon to repair the damage – at precisely the moment when its resources have been constrained and global marketization has limited its sovereignty. Politically, the consequence has been voter frustration, a discrediting of the mixed economy, and a resurrection of pre-Keynesian economics.

There is now an impasse, in which neo-liberalism has not restored jobs and growth, and new social problems have arisen but the old Centre-Left methods of the early postwar era are, in an increasingly global economy, neither feasible nor credible. Yet certain fundamental verities remain. Full employment is still the centrepiece of a decent society. Social partnership remains a necessary instrument of social progress. Trade unionism continues to be the best political means of organizing and mobilizing ordinary people.

Because of globalisation and technological shifts, labour needs increasingly to adapt its skills, and demand for relatively unskilled labour is falling, so that

every nation is experiencing increases in poverty, unemployment and margi-
nalisation depending on its particular institutions. At the same time the terms
and conditions of work for those in employment are deteriorating. The quality
and profile of work is being degraded for the majority while a minority enjoy
increasing privilege. Inequality is universally increasing.

The developments in the labour market have come as the size and power of
deregulated financial institutions and markets have grown internationally and
domestically, and as the penetration of low cost imports has rapidly increased
and the pace of technological innovation has mushroomed. These factors have
combined to lower the demand for relatively unskilled labour across the OECD,
exacerbated in Europe by macroeconomic policies that have remained perversely restrictve even in recession.

In Europe, North America and Australia, slower productivity growth and
reduced GDP growth have translated into inadequate quantities or qualities of
jobs – or both. In Europe, where the welfare state and trade unionism remain
stronger, wages have largely held up but the shortfall has taken the form of
higher unemployment. In the US, though more jobs have been created, a
disproportionate share have been low-wage, often temporary or part-time, with
little or no security, no prospects for advancement and few if any fringe-benefits.
The UK, with the longest stretch of right-wing rule, has had the worst of both
worlds – high unemployment, an erosion of labour rights, and a deterioration
in the quality as well as the quantity of jobs.

The task

Our task is political and economic. We need to re-create the political coalition
that will support the creation of an international financial and trade architecture – a set of domestic policies and new institutional systems that will contest
these trends. We need to reform the public sector and thus to rekindle trust in
it as the necessary instrument of a mixed economy. We need more and better
jobs, a fairer distribution of pre-tax income and an economy that is friendly to
the human and natural world. Growth that is careless of our environment
carries costs as potentially ruinous as unemployment. Neither can the labour
market ignore the family, for it is a central building block in our civilisation
and mothers and fathers alike need access to the labour market on equal terms,
as well as social supports that make it possible to reconcile work and parenting.

The recognition of the shared experience of advanced industrialised countries is central to success – not least because any successful national project
will demand a wholly reformed international architecture and thus collabora-
tion between states. The power of financial markets, the spread of privatisation
and the accent on price stability in macroeconomic policy are part of a wider
global movement in which power and ideas are held by the New Right. They
must be contested internationally if they are to be successfully contested at

home.

There are grounds for optimism. Women, emerging as one of the drivers of the economy, are keenly aware that they need a social infrastrucutre of support if they are to make their lives work. The careless construction of a market society has generated much bitterness – from savers increasingly aware that the inadequate protection of their funds means poverty in old age, to trained workers who can still not find work – which can be husbanded into a progressive coalition. Equally, as the seminar in Magdalen on which this book is based underlined, there are the makings of an international political coalition that is minded to reign in international currency exchanges and set boundaries to markets.

The means

It is important first to assert that any supposed 'natural' rate of unemployment, whether defined as the 'Non-Accelerating Inflation Rate of Unemployment' or as in some other economic theory, should not be regarded as a practical ceiling.

The European Commission's White Paper on Growth, Competitiveness and Employment aims for an unemployment rate of 5% by 2000. In achieving that, macroeconomic policies, althcugh vital, can only go so far. The problem of slow growth and high unemployment is both cyclical *and* structural. The remedy will require labour market policies to improve human skills and to define 'flexibility' in a manner friendly to working families and women, in tandem with Keynesian policies to restore higher levels of investment, productivity, growth and purchasing power.

However, this Keynesianism is much more subtle and ambitious than usually characterised. It aims to increase social investment rather than merely pump-prime; it seeks to restructure the public sector to maximise the employment content of spending; it recognises that without active remediation in the labour market disadvantaged groups will remain so; it knows that it needs to operate within new international rules if it has the remotest chance of success. The world has changed; and Keynesianism must change with it.

Conventional analysis is hobbled by several false dichotomies. Is the problem on the demand side or on the supply side? Does it require greater protection of workers or greater labour market flexibility? Does it require fiscal remedy, or monetary? Macroeconomic expansion or macroeconomic discipline?

Each of these formulations leads up a blind alley. As the White Paper makes clear, 'flexibility' does not mean simply making it easier to fire workers. Affirmative flexibility requires better trained and educated workers, lifelong learning strategies, more dynamic uses of labour-market subsidies and renewed social compacts that allow economies to run closer to full employment without courting inflation. Flexibility requires making it cheaper for industry to hire new workers but without cutting wages. The White Paper sensibly makes the case for switching the burden of taxation away from employment through regressive payroll taxes and onto activity that harms the environment. Flexibility, in our terms, also means more creative approaches to job-sharing, shorter working time, and work arrangement and welfare-state programmes friendlier to parenting needs.

At the same time, job training and 'competitiveness', taken alone, cannot restore full employment as long as excessively tight macroeconomic policies prevail. Indeed, without effective macroeconomic policies, a sole emphasis on human capital solutions will lead only to a better-trained, more frustrated workforce. In America, at least 20% of college graduates have jobs that do not require college degrees; the skills of American workers have been rising while their wages have been stagnant or falling. In Australia, members of the Aboriginal community have complained about being endlessly retrained without being given the means of economic development.

This is not to say that training is not necessary; it is imperative. It is only to say that training, by itself, is insufficient.

As the economist Robert Solow has observed, Europe may suffer from some 'rigidities' in its labour markets, but the more important source of European unemployment is excessively tight monetary policy. The recent American recovery has also been constrained by a premature decision by the Federal Reserve Board to raise interest rates, well short of the restoration of full employment and in the absence of any inflationary pressures.

Macroeconomic policy

An expansionary macroeconomic strategy will entail both a more accommodative monetary policy and a fiscal policy that uses public borrowing directly to finance increased investment. Europe and America both have shortfalls of private investment and high real interest rates. As the Reagan era in the US shows, public deficits used merely as 'demand-side' stimulus do not lead to sustainable growth. Reagan quadrupled the US public debt yet the growth rate remained below the postwar trend. This occurred because the deficits financed primarily private consumption but without leading to increased private investment. At a time of relatively high public debt and structrual budget deficits, further public borrowing can be defended when the proceeds are used to increase investment directly and to lever community projects. Although some European countries have reached the limits of prudent public borrowing, Europe as a whole has further capacity to use public borrowing to finance public investment. Thus we are attracted by the idea of European bonds, whose proceeds would pay for social and infrastructure investments. These could be used both counter-cyclically and as part of an ongoing investment programme.

At the heart of the conventional analysis is a false dichotomy between attacking the structural and cyclical manifestations of the problem. No policies addressed at solving structural issues can succeed if the cyclical conjunction remains adverse, whilst if cyclicial problems remain unsolved they quickly become structural. At the same time, to imagine that structural problems only emerge because of restrictive economic policies that excacerbate economic downturns or that there are no constraints on expansionary macroeconomic policy is equally unhelpful. Policy must attack both dimensions – coherently.

To argue that the limits of expansionary fiscal policy are being approached in Europe is to fall into the trap that Europe's unemployment problem is wholly structural. It is not, and part of the reason why budget deficits are high is because the recession has been so deep and protracted; they are cyclically induced. Savings are some 5 or 6% of GDP higher than investment, implying that 8 or 9 million people are unnecessarily jobless.

To engage in restrictive fiscal policy and to tolerate continued high unemployment, therefore, is to guarantee that structural public deficits will continue. High unemployment reduces public revenues and increases demands for public spending that merely keeps people on the dole and contributes nothing to national wealth. The way to reduce the structural deficit is to increase public borrowing if the proceeds of such borrowing are used to increase investment, productivity and hence employment.

Policy in Europe remains restrictive with real interest rates higher than in similar recessions and countries perversely tightening fiscal policy. A European Keynesian response, spearheaded by a contra-cyclical fund, possibly under independent custodianship, would provide a long overdue stimulus. This could phase back its lending during the upswing, ready to act aggressively in the next downturn. It would also be the flagship for the wider network of investment banks we mention below.

Manufacturing and services

We can no longer rely on manufacturing to supply enough good jobs. The steadily rising productivity that was once the source of rising living standards for ordinary people now produces mass unemployment, while its fruits go to a small financial elite whose main expertise is in the rearrangement of assets. Thus, while lean, efficient manufacturing is desirable to maintain competitiveness, it will not be the source of enough good jobs; indeed, the more productive we become, the more jobs we will wipe out.

Over the long term, human needs are infinite. People displaced from the physical production of goods can be re-employed in the production of other, newly invented goods, or – increasingly – in the service sector.

It was once thought that productivity growth in the service sector was inherently stagnant. As the economist William Baumol observes, a string quartet is no more productive in 1994 than in 1794, though it expects to be paid at 1994 wages. You cannot perform the Minute Waltz more 'productively' by playing it in thirty seconds. Certain other service jobs, such as teacher, waiter and taxi-driver, will have essentially flat productivity growth. Yet in an information economy, most service jobs do in fact have rising productivity. Medical technicians, telephone operators, computer programmers, bank clerks and film editors all do their jobs far more efficiently than even a decade ago thanks to computers.

Even journalists are more productive thanks to word processors!

Rising productivity in services means that prices can drop while wages rise. As prices drop, more people can afford to consume services, just as they could consume more manufactured goods even as manufactured goods continued to pay high wages. Thus services, once considered the stepchildren of the economy, can in fact be the source of good jobs – if we also have an acceptable distribution of income and if we have institutions that force wages to rise as productivity rises. These include strong unions and minimum wages and legislation guaranteeing full benefits to part time and temporary workers. What kind of service sector we have is a political choice. For example, Denmark and the US both have approximately the same fraction of the workforce listed as household workers. In the US, these workers are mostly private servants of the wealthy; in Denmark, they are mostly social providers of home care for the elderly and group child care for the young.

Labour markets and families

At present, there are 35 million people out of work in the OECD nations, while many millions are working far longer hours than they wish. The task is to rearrange those hours so that everyone who wants a job can have one, while parents can have adequate time away from their job without sacrificing job security or standards of pay. The key task is to revise working time, as an opportunity that better attunes the world of work to the demands of parenting and other human needs, rather than merely as a strategy of sharing the pain. The aim should be to make part-time work more attractive to workers, not less attractive to employers.

Beveridge proposed that the welfare state would pay for "interruptions" from work caused by illness, disability or old age. Half a century later, we need a new work-and-welfare state, recognizing that time away from work is normal, necessary and desirable. A work-and-welfare state would subsidise sabbaticals for both training and parenting. It would include not just paid parental leave after a child is born but would also make a somewhat reduced working week the norm for parents of young children, rather than seeing the father as the primary breadwinner and the mother as the primary caregiver. As the American sociologist Arlie Hochschild has observed, only when the division of labour in the household is changed in favour of equal responsibility for keeping house and raising children can we realistically expect a complementary change in the division of labour on the workplace in favour of full gender equality in occupational opportunities, employer expectations and career paths.

Globalisation of finance and trade

As we have noted, the context for the impasse of the mixed, full employment economy is a globalized and substantally deregulated economy. This has many consequences. The footloose multinational corporation undercuts national efforts at economic stabilization. Wage regulation in one country becomes precarious, since private capital can simply migrate to areas of cheaper wages and lesser labour standards. Macroeconomic stimulus in one country is nearly impossible because it invites a run on the national currency.

At the heart of the problem is the deregulation of global finance. Since the collapse of the Bretton Woods regime, the shift to floating exchange rates and the internationalisation of private finance, the real economy has become a hostage to the financial economy. This is a deeper and more fundamental problem for the mixed, social democratic economy than free trade. Swedish Keynesianism, for example, could live perfectly well with free trade. But in a global recession it is threatened by porous, deregulated finance.

It is the interaction of deregulated finance, with its short-term time horizons, demand for high dividend pay-outs and capacity to move anywhere in the world instantaneously, with deregulated labour markets that has raised unemployment rates, undercut labour's bargaining power and reduced the wages paid to unskilled labour. Employers want casualised work in order to manage their wage bills flexibly at every stage in the business cycle and therefore maximise returns to their shareholders.

There have been impressive initiatives in the US to prod financial institutions into serving longer term ends and social goals – and even to finance public investment projects that have, in California for instance, helped to soften the economic downturn. The loan loss experience has been impressive and many small businesses and housing projects have been launched that would otherwise not have happened. At the same time the experience has helped to build support for progressive politics.

But the US remains a market based financial system becoming more market based; and the same is true of Britain, with signs even that mainland Europe is moving in the same direction. This trend is reinforced by the globalisation of finance and the mushrooming of new financial markets in futures and financial deriviatives. Thus, international and domestic financial deregulation are part of the same destructive coin.

At the very least we need to construct a financial system in which networks of public investment banks and regulation on the German model permits different financial priorities to be expressed across a range of activities, from housing to small businesses, through financing counter-cyclical infrastucture spending, to community development.

Yet this will be very difficult in the prevailing financial climate. Some progress, as in the US, is possible; but without stabilising the massive short-term financial flows between industrialised countries and the markets they rest upon, the system will continue to be market based. As a result, the transaction costs of speculative financial trading need to be sharply increased by taxation and prudential regulation.

This will require global participation because of the 'free rider' problem; and one obvious building block is Europe. The re-establishment of the ERM with the dollar and yen as a global system of managed currencies is one possibility; another is common, tough regulatory standards for all European banks who operate in the financial futures markets. Taken together and with sufficient will, the means exist to reinvent the financial architecture in which domestic and international Keynesian policies become possible again.

Trade and labour

While we generally favour open trade, we also recognize that in a world of very high unemployment, footloose capital and wildly divergent standards of pay and of regulation, laissez-faire trade can have the effect of pulling down standards and pay scales in the advanced countries. Our task is to help bring poor countries up to the levels of rich ones – not vice versa. That task will not be attained by having the OECD countries emulate the pay scales and labour conditions of the third world. Nor will it even help workers in third world countries.

Most of us favour conditional free trade – mediated through such institutions as social charters or social tariffs. Governments pursue free trade policies for the welfare benefits it should produce. Labour standard legislation is intended to ensure that there is no deflationary bias to the system (due to low wages reducing purchasing power) and that the benefits are equally distributed. Nations that desire to be full members of the free trade system need to agree to its rules. Just as these include an emerging code of rules on such issues as market access, subsidies and intellectual property protection, they must also include rules on minimal labour standards and environmental protection. Otherwise we risk a global race to the bottom that undercuts hard won standards in the advanced countries. Nations that wish to retain child and prison labour and to deny rights of association and collective bargaining are free to do so – but they should not expect laissez-faire access to the markets of nations that believe in a higher level of social decency.

The practical opportunity to achieve this goal presents itself in the new World Trade Organization. We should strive for the inclusion of a social charter that defines basic labour rights and then add specific elements later on, once the fundamental principle and procedure are established.

The third sector

One consistent theme in three days of talks at Magdalen was the potential of the voluntary sector and a redesigned public sector to make important contributions in their own right to job generation. The public sector could more self-consciously set out to improve the labour content of its spending, while the voluntary sector is well able to absorb more workers.

The constraint on both is finance, and some of the proposals listed above might redress this issue. This third sector has the capacity to be an employer offering quality and fulfilling work that is socially useful.

Trade unions

Equally, trade unions are key components in any progressive coalition. Properly constituted and organised, they offer the means of contesting the trends in wage inequality, redefining notions of 'wage flexiblity', and demonstrating that democratic institutions in civil society can improve not only work but the quality of life. They can be the champions of a mixed economy, the advocates of a better life for all but the independently wealthy, and the mobilisers of widespread political participation. Trade unions can mediate the idea of a better, more fulfilling, working world.

Women as an economic force

The emerging power of women in the economy (as described by Linda Tarr-Whelan in Chapter 7) can be the principal engine of a renewed growth process, provided that they are enabled properly to participate by the necessary infrastructure of support. Politically, their own mobilization makes women increasingly sympathetic to the progressive/social democratic cause. Without a 'gender gap' among working women in favour of Bill Clinton in the 1992 American election, he would not have been elected.

The growth of the female workforce is common across all OECD states, so that female participation rates nearly equal those of men. However, there tends to be little overlap, with only some 9% of women working in 'men's jobs' in the US. At the same time, less than 10% of women now expect to spend their life in the home. Yet there is still a significant gender-based wage gap in most OECD countries.

Women invest more in their education and at every level of the jobs scale are increasingly regarded as more skilled and adaptable. The service sector in particular has found women more employable and productive at the wage rates offered, and with promising prospects for service sector employment, so the role of women, already important, is set to grow.

Yet the marriage of work and family places impossible demands upon women, who are responding in a number of ways. An increasing number of small business start-ups are by women, with success rates 5 times higher than men in the US – in part to flee male corporate hierarchies and in part to have more control over work and family time. Equally, women are the fastest growing element in trade union membership.

Despite the importance of the gender gap in his election, President Clinton has yet to deliver on his campaign promises to provide an infrastructure of family support, in particular for child care. Yet freeing women to play a more active economic role holds out hope for wealth creation in the round, so that strategies for supporting female employment, parenting and the interface between work and family are socially and economically efficient. For the Left, women also offer a key political constituency.

The politics

The construction of an effective political coalition defines the economic task. Unless parties of the Left can mobilise popular support for their project with an effective popular narrative, they will neither win nor sustain power while they implement their programme. Thus, developing economic ideas without continually relating them to how they serve mass economic interests and accomodate real trends in our economies and societies is a nonsense. Hence the importance of incorporating women and their agenda into the heart of political and economic thinking; of redesigning political and economic institutions to work with rather than against those changes; and also of exploiting rather than protesting at the trends that are driving all our economies to have a higher service sector content. Revived trade unions and increased female participation together offer an historic opportunity for reshaping employment models.

The Magdalen seminar suggested a number of intriguing new elements of a progressive coalition. There should be a continuation of this promising beginning.

International seminar on growth and employment

Between 13-15 April 1994, at Magdalen College, Oxford, around 40 senior policy advisers from the leading progressive and social democratic think tanks, universities and trade unions in Europe, North America and Australia met with the aim of exchanging and developing ideas on the key issues of growth and employment.

The seminar was sponsored by five organisations: the Center for Policy Alternatives (US); the Economic Policy Institute (US); the Friedrich Ebert Foundation (Germany); the Fabian Society (UK); and UNISON, the UK public service union.

The style was deliberately informal and private.

We are particularly grateful to Will Hutton and Bob Kuttner who acted as Rapporteurs and burnt the midnight oil to write the statement of the seminar's conclusions (produced in chapter 9). It is something of a call to arms, recognising that the commonality of our experience across the advanced economies suggests similar roots, and that, despite national variations there is a systemic problem that cannot be solved by a single nation acting alone.

We intend the statement to be used widely as a basis for developing both ideas and common action. The friendships established at the seminar give hope that a live network has been created.

We are grateful to Jacques Delors, President of the European Union, for agreeing to write a preface. This also signals our determination to take up the challenge he has raised to place full employment at the centre of a new agenda for political and economic renewal.

Peter Morris, UNISON

- **AUSTRALIA**
  Peter Botsman

  Evatt Foundation
  Level 6, 677 Sussex St., Sydney, NSW 2000
  Tel: 010 612 261 4766
  Fax: 010 612 261 4835

- **CANADA**
  Duncan Cameron

  Canadian Centre for Policy Alternatives
  804-251 ouest Laurier Ave. West,
  Ottawa, Ontario, K1P 5J6
  Tel: 010 613 563 1341
  Fax: 010 613 233 1458

  Margie Mendell

  Karl Polanyi Institute of Political Economy,
  Concordia University, Montreal, Quebec
  Fax: 010 514 848 2577

- **EUROPE**
  Lutz Belmann

  Institut Arbeitsmark-und-Berufsforschung
  der Bundesanstalt fuer Arbeit
  Regensburger Str. 104, 90327 Nuremberg
  Tel: 010 499 111 793 258

  Chris Boyd

  Jacques Delors' cabinet
  100 rue de la Loi, 1049 Brussels
  Tel: 010 322 295 9639
  Fax: 010 322 295 3222

  Peter Coldrick

  European TUC
  International Trade Union House,
  Bd. Emile Jacqmain 155, 1210 Brussels
  Tel: 010 322 224 0443
  Fax: 010 322 224 0454

  Gerard Collomb

  Fondation Jean Jaures
  73 avenue Paul Doumer, F-75116, Paris
  Tel: 010 331 407 22121
  Fax: 010 331 407 22139

  Karl Duffek

  Karl Renner Institute
  Khleslplatz 12, A-1125 Vienna
  Tel: 010 431 804 65010
  Fax: 010 431 804 0874

  John Evans

  TUAC-OECD
  26 avn. de la grande armee, F-75017, Paris
  Tel: 010 331 4763 6263
  Fax: 010 331 4754 9828

Georg Fischer	*Adviser to the Austrian Minister of Finance* Private Office, Minister of Finance Himmelpfortgasse 8, A-1010 Vienna Tel: 010 431 514 33 1377 Fax: 010 431 513 9888
David Foden	*European Trade Union Institute* International Trade Union House, Bd. Emile Jacqmain 155, 1210 Brussels Tel: 010 322 224 0470 Fax: 010 322 224 0502
Heinz-Albert Huthmacher	*Friedrich Ebert Foundation, German Office* D-53170 Bonn, Godesberger Allee 149 Tel: 010 49 228 88 33 69 Fax: 010 49 228 88 35 38
Jan Karlsson	*Political Adviser to Alan Larsson MP* Riksdagen, S-100 12 Stockholm Tel: 010 46 821 1524
Vera Mathias	*Fondation Jean Jaures* q.v.
Karl-Peter Schackmann-Fallis	*Head of General Secretary's Office, SPD* SPD Parteivorstand, Ollenhauerstra 1, 53175 Bonn Tel: 010 49 228 532378 Fax: 010 49 228 532410
Sven Eric Soder	*Olof Palme International Centre* Drottninggatan 86, Box 3221, S-10364, Stockholm Tel: 010 468 210739 Fax: 010 468 102375

- **UK**

Edward Balls	*Economic Adviser to Gordon Brown MP* House of Commons, London, SW1A 0AA Tel: 0171 219 3000
Rodney Bickerstaffe	*UNISON* Civic House, 20 Grand Depot Rd., London, SE18 6SF Tel: 0181 854 2244 Fax: 0181 316 7770

Nick Butler	*BP* Britannic House, 1 Finsbury Circus, London, EC2M 7BA Tel: 0171 496 4095 Fax: 0171 496 4099
Sir Alec Cairncross	*Economic Adviser* St.Peter's College, Oxford
Dan Corry	*Institute for Public Policy Research* 30-32 Southampton St., London, WC2E 7RA Tel: 0171 379 9400 Fax: 0171 497 0373
Rita Donaghy	*UNISON* q.v.
Dan Finn	*Unemployment Unit* 409 Brixton Rd., London, SW9 7DG Tel: 0171 737 0818 Fax: 0171 326 0818
Andrew Graham	*Balliol College, Oxford* Broad St., Oxford, OX1 3DJ Tel: 0865 277765 Fax: 0865 277803
Paul Gregg	*National Insititute for* *Economic and Social Research* 2 Dean Trench St., London, SW1P 3HE Tel: 0171 222 7665 Fax: 0171 222 1435
Will Hutton	*The Guardian* 119 Farringdon St., London, EC1R Tel: 0171 833 4456 Fax: 0171 278 2332
Bill Keegan	*The Observer* q.v. The Guardian
David Lea	*Trade Union Congress* Congress House, Great Russell St., London, WC1B 3LS Tel: 0171 636 4030 Fax: 0171 636 0632

Emma MacLennan	*MacLennan Ward Associates* 40 Pendle Rd., London, SW16 6RU Tel: 0181 769 6789
Peter Morris	*UNISON* q.v.
Geoff Mulgan	*DEMOS* 9 Bridewell Place, London, EC4V 6AP Tel: 0171 353 4479 Fax: 0171 353 4481
Stephen Pollard	*Fabian Society* 11 Dartmouth St., London, SW1H 9BN Tel: 0171 222 8877 Fax: 0171 976 7153
John Prescott MP	*Deputy Leader of the Labour Party* House of Commons, London, SW1A 0AA Tel: 0171 219 3000 Fax: 0171 219 6976
Derek Robinson	*Magdalen College, Oxford* & *Institute of Economics and Statistics* St. Cross Building, Manor Rd., Oxford 0X1 3UL Tel: 0865 271064 Fax: 0865 271094
Glenys Thornton	*Political Consultant* 40 Lavender Grove, London, E8 3LS Tel: 0171 275 8488 Fax: 0171 923 2243
Roland Wales	*Head of Policy, Labour Party* 150 Walworth Rd., London, SE17 1JT Tel: 0171 701 1234 Fax: 0171 701 6327
David Ward	*MacLennan Ward Associates* 40 Pendle Rd., London, SW16 6RU Tel: 0181 769 6789

- **USA**

Eileen Appelbaum	*Economic Policy Institute* 1730 Rhode Island Avenue NW, Suite 200 Washington DC 20036 Tel: 0101 202 775 8810 Fax: 0101 202 775 0819
Jeff Faux	*Economic Policy Institute* q.v.
Richard Ferlauto	*Center for Policy Alternatives* 1875 Connecticut Avenue NW, Suite 710 Washington DC 20009 Tel: 0101 202 387 6030 Fax: 0101 202 986 2539
Heidi Hartmann	*Institute for Women's Policy Research* 1400 20th St. NW, Washington DC 20036 Tel: 0101 202 785 5100 Fax: 0101 202 833 4362
Robert Kuttner	*American Prospect* 146 Mount Auburn St., Cambridge, Massachusetts 02138 Tel: 0101 617 547 2950 Fax: 0101 617 547 3896
Walter Russell Mead	*World Policy Institute* 1217 Royal St., New Orleans, Louisiana 70116 Tel: 0101 504 524 8648 Fax: 0101 504 529 1105
Keith Tarr-Whelan	*Tarr-Whelan and Associates* 3626 N. Kensington St., Arlington, Virginia 22207 Tel: 0101 703 536 5145 Fax: 0101 703 532 0881
Linda Tarr-Whelan	*Center for Policy Alternatives* q.v.

All telephone numbers are as from the UK.

Contributors

Chris Boyd works in the Cabinet of Jacques Delors, President of the European Commission, as an adviser in Brussels.

Jacques Delors is President of the European Commission in Brussels

John Evans is General Secretary of the Trade Union Advisory Committee to the Organisation for Economic Co-operation and Development in Paris.

Jeff Faux is President of the Economic Policy Institute in Washington DC.

Richard C. Ferlauto is Public Capital Program Manager with the Center for Policy Alternatives in Washington D.C.

Andrew Graham is a Fellow and Tutor in Economics at Balliol College, Oxford.

Will Hutton is Economics Editor of *The Guardian* in London and was Joint Rapporteur of the International Seminar on Growth and Employment at Magdalen College, Oxford in April 1994.

Robert Kuttner is Editor of *The American Prospect* in Boston and was Joint Rapporteur of the International Seminar on Growth and Employment at Magdalen College, Oxford in April 1994.

Stephen Pollard is Editor of *Fabian Review* and Research Officer of the Fabian Society in London.

Linda Tarr-Whelan is President of the Center for Policy Alternatives in Washington D.C.